P9-BIW-699

AUGUSTANA UNIVERSITY COLLEGE
LIBRARY

ARE THESE THE WORDS OF JESUS?

Dramatic Evidence from beyond the New Testament

IAN WILSON

Lennard Publishing
1990

Heaven and earth will pass away,

but my words will never pass away.

Matthew 24:35

LENNARD PUBLISHING
a division of Lennard Books Ltd.
Musterlin House
Jordan Hill Road
Oxford OX2 8DP

British Library Cataloguing in Publication Data
is available for this title.

ISBN 1 85291 086 0

First published 1990
© Ian Wilson, 1990

This book is copyright under the Berne Convention.
No reproduction without permission. All rights reserved.

Phototypeset in Monotype Plantin.
Design by Forest Publication Services, Luton.
Cover design by Pocknell & Co.
Reproduced, printed and bound in Great Britain by
Butler & Tanner Ltd, Frome and London

Contents

AUGUSTANA UNIVERSITY COLLEGE
LIBRARY

Text Figures

Author's Preface and Acknowledgements

This book would probably never have been written without an express invitation for me to do so from publisher Mark Booth. Mark had commissioned one of my earlier books, *The After Death Experience*, and after he moved to Lennard Books he suggested to me the theme, 'Are These the Words of Jesus?', the original concept being a compendium of all the apocryphal and similarly non-canonical sayings attributed to Jesus, for which I would simply write a few thousand words of introduction.

Such material was already broadly familiar to me from a previous project, *Jesus: The Evidence*, so the assignment was an easy one to accept. However, it was some while before I could take up the project, and although by this time Mark Booth had left Lennard Books, his co-publisher Roderick Brown continued with the same encouragement.

But once into the project it quickly became apparent that the book would be a very dull one indeed if it remained just a collection of apocrypha and other claimed sayings of Jesus. Since the great majority of apocryphal works richly merit the more pejorative sense of the term apocrypha, and are often both long and tedious, to present lengthy portions of such documents only to dismiss them for their spuriousness seemed of no great benefit to any reader.

Accordingly a far better approach appeared to be to concentrate on those comparatively few documents that have some reasonably serious claim to incorporating otherwise unrecorded words once spoken by Jesus, or have some related interest value. And this I have tried to do, with particular attention to some of the more recent manuscript discoveries, such as the Nag Hammadi Gospel of Thomas, and the Mar Saba 'Secret Gospel'. In accord with the original concept, full texts of many of the more interesting documents are included in the book's Appendix.

Even so, this is not intended to be an exhaustive approach to the subject, and I have sought in the main to provide an updated and popular synthesis of previous approaches such as M.R. James's still unsurpassed *The Apocryphal New Testament*, Roderic Dunkerley's *Beyond the Gospels*, R.M. Grant and D.M. Freedman's *The Secret Sayings of Jesus*, and Morton Smith's *The Secret Gospel*, to all of which I am indebted in a variety of ways. Where a translation has been couched in artificial 'Authorised Version' Biblical English, I have usually taken the liberty of updating this into modern English. In addition I am indebted to Thomas O'Lambdin's translation of the Nag Hammadi Gospel of Thomas, as published in J.M. Robinson's *The Nag Hammadi Library in English*; and Morton Smith's translation of the Mar Saba 'Secret Gospel'. For quotations from the canonical New Testament I have usually relied on the ever lucid and dignified English of the *Jerusalem Bible*.

One final thankyou is a posthumous one. Throughout this book there keeps recurring the name of Bishop Eusebius of Caesarea, author of a *History of the Church* written around 325 AD. In the early part of his life Eusebius became caught up in times that were particularly turbulent for Christians, and showed that he was certainly not made of the stuff of martyrs. As a writer he was not particularly literary, nor can he rank in the topmost flight of the world's historians. But in the course of his book he quoted from, or summarised, often at considerable length, more than one hundred ancient sources, many of which were already old in his time, and have since become otherwise completely lost to us. Without his patient scholarship all those years ago, both this book and our whole knowledge of Christianity's formative years would be very much the poorer.

Bristol, England June 1989

Introduction: The Significance of Jesus

Whatever our religious persuasion may be, it is an inescapable fact that in all history no-one has had a greater impact on the western world than Jesus Christ. The towers and spires of churches and cathedrals built in his name still command something of the skylines of our towns and cities, despite the recent fierce competition from high-rise office-blocks. Our major annual festivals, even that most aggressively commercial one called Christmas, denote events from Jesus's life. The calendrical dates we almost unthinkingly use on every letter and newspaper hark back to some form of approximation of the year of his birth. If we give evidence in a law court we will take an oath of truthfulness by holding in our hands a book enshrining his words. The day of the week on which most of us rest is one designated through sixteen centuries as set aside for his worship. Throughout history millions of lives have been changed, shaped and guided by his teachings. Some of our greatest works of art and literature are those that have derived inspiration from him, or been devoted to his memory. In the words of former Cambridge University ancient history professor T.R. Glover, Jesus's influence is 'the most striking and outstanding fact in history .... There is no figure in human history that signifies more'.

Yet the irony is that of himself Jesus left nothing that could be construed as physically permanent. Although he was said to have been a carpenter, he left no known building, or even part of one, to be preserved and admired as the work of his human hands. While innumerable great cathedrals and churches with the costliest of fitments have been erected by those who called themselves his followers, there is not a whit to suggest he ever wanted such permanence or magnificence. Because of the very manner of his apparent leaving of this world, there are not, nor, it seems, ever have been, any physical remains of his one-time human body that can today be venerated at some lofty pyramid or sumptuous tomb.

For in essence, apart from that brief moment when he was flesh and blood on earth, all there ever has been or can be to Jesus is the Word. How easy that is to say, how difficult to understand! Of course we have absolutely no known means of recapturing, even if we could understand them, the exact sounds of the words that fell from his lips onto the air of Galilee and Jerusalem two thousand years ago. And although his followers went to great lengths to preserve on paper something of what they remembered of his sayings in the form of the canonical gospels, what we have from these after all these years can only be an imperfect rendition, limited not least by having had to be translated into modern languages.

Yet even so, for world-wide millions of Jesus's followers those words have been supremely, life-changingly important. They may have absolutely no substance that can lend itself to any form of chemical analysis. They may have absolutely no power that can ever be understood in terms of the laws of physics. Yet they have been words that men and women in their millions have wanted to live by, and to die by...

And inevitably all this raises the question: If the words of this one man enshrined in just four slim gospels can mean so much, and have been responsible for so much, do those gospels represent the sum total of all that is known of what he said? It stands to reason that in Jesus's lifetime he must have uttered publicly a great deal more than the four gospel writers alone can possibly have written down. So, have any of these words been preserved anywhere else, in any surviving form? This is the central question of our book.

Chapter 1

'But My Words Will Never Pass Away...'

Just a single passage, in a single gospel (John's), is all that represents Jesus as having ever set anything down in writing. Brought before him had been a woman caught in the unlawful act of sexual intercourse with a man not her husband. As a notable rabbi of the time, Jesus was expected to condemn this woman to what his native religion decreed as her appropriate punishment: death by stoning. Asked if this was indeed his judgement, Jesus's first response was merely to scrawl with his finger in the dust. Pressed for a reply, he responded: 'If there is one of you who has never sinned, let him be the first to throw a stone at her.' (John 8:7), after which he resumed his scrawling in the dust. Although whatever he may have written in that moment has gone unrecorded, inevitably it must very soon have been obliterated by the wind and by the trampling of feet.

Now there is a whole world of meaning even in just this single, ostensibly simple incident recorded of Jesus. More than a thousand years before, in the time of the prophet Moses, the commandments of Jesus's people's God were said to have been somehow graven on hard stone tablets: tangible, ostensibly everlasting words, including a specific ruling on adultery, that generations of Jews had carried around with them in their Ark of the Covenant, and had tried to follow in their daily lives. Yet when asked to ratify even a single seemingly straightforward one of these rock-hard commandments Jesus, whom some would call the Son of the Living God, simply scrawled in the dust. Was it that in this action he was pointing to the insubstantiality of any too hard-and-fast rules of life? That all matter is dust, and to dust it shall return? That ultimately all that truly matters, and is truly everlasting, is the perpetually insubstantial spirit of love?

In such a light it is tempting to believe that it was with this very same mentality that Jesus quite deliberately chose, as he certainly did, not to leave behind any of his words written down in any so permanent and committing form as by his own hand. This is one of the many extraordinary ironies of Christianity, that its founder, who was described as reading in the synagogue in the incident described in Luke 4:16–20, and therefore was quite definitely literate, to the best of our knowledge accorded to posterity not a single formal document of his own writing or even of his own dictation. Despite living among a people who set great store by the written word, there has never ever been a hint that Jesus might have left anything set on parchment or paper, and duly notarised 'This is the authentic teaching of Jesus of Nazareth', for his followers to mould their lives by.

Now it cannot be that the surprise of Jesus's arrest and execution prevented his arranging anything of this kind, for the gospels make quite clear that he anticipated these events well before they happened, and virtually orchestrated their timing.

Also it cannot be that he did not intend his utterances to be preserved. According to Matthew's gospel he quite specifically said 'Heaven and earth will pass away, but my words will never pass away,' (Matthew 24:35). He taught, as if for repeated use, at least one specific prayer, the Lord's Prayer of Matthew 6:9–13 and Luke 11:2–4. And modern textual studies of the gospels have revealed much to suggest that he formulated his sayings and parables in ways to ensure they would be easily memorised, and suffer as little distortion as possible.

We must therefore face the fact that Jesus quite deliberately intended that his words should be preserved, but that they should be conveyed and reconveyed only indirectly. Effectively it is as if he wanted them to be prey to the human frailties and imperfections of being passed on by others. Yet while this is undeniable, it should not be construed as any form of attempt to diminish or downgrade the value of the books of 'Evangelia', or 'Good News', that have come down to us as the gospels accredited to Matthew,

Mark, Luke and John. These have been accepted by Christians from as early as the second century as *the* prime source of our knowledge of all that Jesus said and did. As already emphasised, they have been an incalculable source of daily inspiration to literally hundreds of millions of Jesus's followers up to and including our own time, and there can be no question of their faithfulness to the spirit of what Jesus once taught.

But as has been made clear by numerous scholarly studies during the last century and a half, any idea that all these books derive from totally unimpeachable, first-hand eyewitness reporting simply does not bear serious scrutiny. From the well-established methods of literary criticism it is now recognised and commonly accepted among scriptural scholars that Mark's gospel, despite being the least valued by the early Church, was the earliest of the three so-called synoptic gospels, and was used as a framework by the authors of the Matthew and Luke gospels. Since even the early Church did not seem to recognise Mark as any immediate disciple of Jesus, but instead as some form of secretary or interpreter to the disciple Peter, serious questions have been raised as to whether the author of the Matthew gospel, who was undeniably dependent on the Mark gospel, could possibly have been the Matthew who was the tax-collector disciple of Jesus. After all, any true immediate disciple would hardly have had any wish or need to use the work of one who was not. Similarly the author of the Luke gospel, in his very opening sentence, freely acknowledged the second-hand nature of his creation:

> ... many others have undertaken to draw up accounts of the events that have taken place among us exactly *as these were handed down to us by those who from the outset were eyewitnesses* ... I in my turn ... have decided to write an ordered account ... [italics mine]
>
> (Luke 1:1–4)

As for the John gospel, according to the Church's own early traditions, this was the last gospel to be written, and while its author's account of the events of Jesus's Crucifixion has serious claim to eyewitness testimony, there is much less confidence concerning the lengthy discourses he ascribes to Jesus. For well over a century some New Testament scholars have thought these to derive from a markedly later and less first-hand theology.

Now these very imperfections and uncertainties associated with the canonical gospels only serve to highlight a yet more fundamental area of interest. This is evident not least in the very passage just reproduced from Luke, that 'many others have undertaken to draw up accounts of the events that have taken place among us ...'. While familiarity with the 'famous four' gospels has led to widespread supposition that they were the only near contemporary chronicles of Jesus, effectively Luke tells us that even in Luke's early time there had been at least several previous attempts at the same, suggestive that there may even have been whole gospels that more directly recorded Jesus's words, yet have not survived the passage of centuries.

As already remarked, it is of course a matter of common sense that Jesus must have both said and done a great deal more than we have recorded in the canonical gospels. The leading New Testament scholar Canon Burnett Streeter once calculated that with the exception of the forty days and forty nights in the wilderness, virtually everything else recorded of Jesus in the gospels could be compressed into three weeks, leaving by far the greater part of his life unchronicled. The author of the John gospel concluded his account with the percipient, albeit rather exaggerated words:

> There were many other things Jesus did: if all were written down, the world itself, I suppose, would not hold all the books that would have to be written.
>
> (John 21:25)

But the key question is whether there have been, and/or survive somewhere to this day, records of utterances of Jesus quite independent of the canonical gospels, yet potentially fully authenticable. And there are in fact a variety of pointers to such sayings.

For instance, in Acts Chapter 20, Paul is described as asking an audience of citizens from Ephesus to remember Jesus's words: 'There is more happiness in giving than receiving' (Acts 20:35). The interest here is that although this saying is so readily characteristic of Jesus, it occurs in no known surviving gospel. It is also noteworthy that Paul, who is reliably thought never to have known the human Jesus, most likely delivered his speech to the Ephesians around AD 57 – in all probability, therefore, before a single one of the canonical gospels had come to be written.[1]

The resultant inference is that Paul had access to at least one set of collected sayings of Jesus predating the canonical gospels. Other clues to this come from the way, in chapter 7 of his first letter to the Corinthians, Paul carefully distinguished his own pronouncements from those of Jesus:

> For the married I have something to say, and this is not from me but from the Lord: a wife must not leave her husband ... nor must a husband send his wife away.
>
> (I Corinthians 7:10)

Paul followed this with the statement:

> The rest is from me and not from the Lord.
>
> (I Corinthians 7:12)

when going on to set out certain specific guidelines for Christians who were married to unbelievers. So if Paul could be as definite as this, he had to be already in possession of some formal document of Jesus's teaching.

Quite independently a preserved extract from the otherwise lost writings of the second-century Church historian Papias remarks that Jesus's tax-collector disciple Matthew:

> compiled the Sayings (Logia) in the Aramaic language, and everyone translated them as well as he could.[2]

The interest value of this statement is that it conveys the quite crucial information that while the original tax-collector Matthew apparently genuinely did assemble a form of gospel, it was written in his native Aramaic, the same language as that spoken by Jesus.

It seems also to have consisted mainly if not entirely of a compilation of sayings. Since what we now have as the canonical gospel of Matthew was composed in Greek, and went some way towards a biography of Jesus instead of just sayings, clearly the canonical Matthew gospel, as we have already suspected, must be by a less immediate hand.

Of course this does not exclude the possibility that the eyewitness Matthew's collection of sayings was translated into Greek and embodied, possibly in its entirety, into the gospel that has traditionally carried Matthew's name. But the fascinating feature is that circulating in the first century there must have been at least one document of sayings of Jesus genuinely collected at first hand by an immediate disciple, that has not, at least in its original form, come down to us.

Nor is this likely to have been the only one. The scholars who so painstakingly deduced that the Matthew and Luke authors drew some of their material from Mark also deduced that Matthew and Luke had another common, but non-surviving source, a hypothetical Greek or possibly Aramaic document that has been given the reference name 'Q'. 'Q's existence can be inferred, and something of its original content deduced, from those passages in which the Matthew and Luke gospels show a close similarity to each other, but not to anything in Mark. It seems to have consisted of a number of sayings, plus passages on John the Baptist, and the Temptation in the Wilderness.

The existence of another source, 'M', has been inferred from certain passages exclusive to the canonical Matthew gospel. It can even be deduced that this 'M' is most likely to have been in Aramaic. And the author of the Luke gospel seems similarly to have had some exclusive Aramaic source - Proto-Luke? - from which he obtained some of his information.[3]

In fact the derivation of at least the three synoptic gospels from such primitive assemblages of sayings, together with perhaps collections of parables, miracle stories, etc., is quite evident even from the most cursory study. Early in Mark's gospel is introduced an attention-getting collection of miracle-stories, followed in the fourth chapter by a collection of parables, followed by a sprinkling of more miracle stories. The second half of his Chapter 9 consists of a string of sayings, followed in Chapter 13 by a further clutch of sayings, this time relating to the Second Coming. Whoever wrote or edited the Matthew gospel also drew on another set of sayings, possibly the one compiled by the original tax-collector Matthew, for the famous Sermon on the Mount. Whoever composed the Luke gospel seems to have used this same source in quite different settings for his Chapters 6 and 13.

Accordingly, as long recognised by theologians of the 'Form-Criticism' school, the synoptic gospels comprise substantial chunks of arguably original material, in the form of sayings and doings, joined up by later biographically-inclined editors with the use of weak and often unconvincing 'link-passages' such as 'He left that place...', 'As he was leaving the Temple...', etc.[4]

This hypothesised original form of the gospel material as mere collections of sayings, and similar, is in fact precisely what we would expect of Jewish authorship which, as in the later Talmud, always tended to neglect details of biographical interest. This is in marked contrast to the Gentile world of Jesus's first century where there flourished such great Roman biographers as Plutarch, Suetonius, and Tacitus. So it is from individuals at least partly rooted in this latter tradition that we can expect at least something of the formulation of the gospels in their canonical form to have sprung.

All this leads us to the conclusion that the surviving canonical gospels of Matthew, Mark, Luke and John do not necessarily represent the sum of all that should have been or would have been recorded of Jesus in or near his time. And quite aside from the source gospels, such as 'Q' and Matthew's 'Sayings', the great Church fathers of the centuries immediately following Jesus's lifetime attest to other early sources that may have included some otherwise unknown sayings authentic to Jesus.

For instance, around the end of the second century the theologian Clement of Alexandria mentions several times in his writings a 'Gospel of the Egyptians', quoting from this apparent sayings of Jesus that have no counterparts in the canonical gospels.[5] Although in the third century Clement's fellow-Alexandrian Origen spoke harshly of the writers of this gospel, as having undertaken their task 'rashly, without the needful gifts of grace',[6] even so, is it likely that this gospel's purported sayings of Jesus could all have been total fabrications?

In the fourth century the great St Jerome, responsible for translating our standard Bible into Latin, mentioned 'the Gospel which the Nazarenes and Ebionites use,' commenting that this is called by many (or most) people the original of Matthew.[7]

There is very little surviving information on the Nazarenes and Ebionites, but both are known to have been groups of Jewish Christians, living away from the mainstream of the increasingly Gentile form that Christianity took within decades of its inception. According to the second-century Church father Irenaeus, the Ebionites took daily baths for purification, and used unleavened bread and water for their Eucharist. According to Eusebius, while they greatly revered Christ, they regarded him as 'the child of a normal union between a man and Mary'.[8]

But perhaps the most distinctive feature about the Ebionites as Christians was that they were very Jewish, in this regard quite naturally preferring to have their gospel in the Aramaic language which Jesus and his disciples had spoken, rather than the Greek in which the received canonical gospels came to be written. Although they died out early on, their Aramaic gospel may well therefore have been, as St Jerome suggested it was, our hypothesised collection of 'Sayings' gathered by the original tax-collector Matthew. This would therefore be of priceless importance if one day a copy could be found.

Another indication of the one-time existence of this Aramaic version of Matthew comes from the *Church History* of Bishop Eusebius of Caesarea who mentions of the second-century

Christian missionary St Pantaenus:

> ... he went as far as India, where he appears to have found that Matthew's gospel had arrived before him and was in the hands of some there who had come to know Christ. Bartholomew, one of the apostles, had preached to them and left behind Matthew's account in the actual Aramaic characters, and it was preserved till the time of Pantaenus's mission.[9]

There are also several references, in the writings of Irenaeus, of Eusebius of Caesarea, and of the fourth-century Cypriot Bishop Epiphanius, as well as Clement of Alexandria and Jerome, to an early 'Gospel of the Hebrews' that may or may not have been one and the same as the version of Matthew used by the Nazarenes and Ebionites. According to Eusebius, writing of those books (including Revelation), whose canonicity was disputed in his time:

> ... some have found a place in the list for the 'Gospel of the Hebrews', a book which has a special appeal for those Hebrews who have accepted Christ.[10]

Again, some of the above-mentioned Church fathers quoted from this gospel purported sayings of Jesus that are otherwise unknown from the canonical gospels.

Additionally there are known to have been in existence in the early centuries certain 'gospels' and other works that may have included sayings of Jesus, authentic or otherwise, but which for the most part have long been lost because they were condemned as apocryphal. At the end of the fifth century a 'List of Books to be Accepted and Not to be Accepted' was drawn up that has usually but misleadingly been called by historians the *Decretum Gelasianum*, even though it owed nothing to Pope Gelasius (AD 492–96). The list, which has survived,[10] included gospels under the names of Matthias, Barnabas, Peter, Thomas, Bartholomew and Andrew, a 'Book concerning the birth of the Saviour, and Mary' (also known as the 'Book of the Midwife'), a 'Book concerning the Infancy of the Saviour', together with Acts under the names of the apostles Andrew, Thomas, Peter and Philip.

Such was the thoroughness of early persecutions that many of these, whatever their worth, have failed to survive. But from some, quotations, inclusive of purported sayings of Jesus, have been preserved in the writings of early Church fathers. And of others, again inclusive of purported sayings of Jesus, fragmentary and not so fragmentary portions have come to light among the caches of early manuscripts that continue to be turned up, archaeologically and otherwise, from time to time.

Accordingly, aside from all the sayings and doings of Jesus that must be considered irretrievably lost, there is genuinely quite a substantial body of written material, from a variety of sources, including ones not so far mentioned, that incorporate words at least attributed to Jesus, and that just conceivably *might* have once been uttered by him.

The key question hangs, inevitably, on just how far any of such words can or should be considered authentic. Given the proliferation of early Christian heresies and apocrypha, we must expect a lot of detritus, with comparatively few gems. But even to be able to add any new sayings to those incorporated in the New Testament has to be a most fascinating and worthwhile exercise in its own right. Accordingly our first step will be to consider something of the criteria we need in order to begin at last to answer the key question: are these *really* words that can be believed to have come from the lips of Jesus?

Chapter 2

Learning to Recognise Jesus's Words

In order to evaluate properly the authenticity or otherwise of words alleged to have been spoken by Jesus, one first essential is to have some very clear idea of just who the human Jesus was. Whatever our attitude towards the religion that carries his name, we need to build up some form of 'feel' for the flesh-and-blood individual who walked the paths of Galilee and the streets of Jerusalem nearly two thousand years ago.

In this regard, perhaps we should not be too surprised that there should be some claims that Jesus never even existed. In the last two decades G.A. Wells, Professor of German at Birkbeck College, London, has written no less than three seemingly erudite books [1] on this theme, essentially arguing that because Paul's letter can be demonstrated to have been written before the gospels, the gospel writers must simply have invented a human Jesus to fit Paul's imaginings. Similarly, around the same time that Wells first aired his ideas, Manchester University Oriental Studies specialist John Allegro launched the view that Christianity began as a secret cult of the sacred mushroom, with the name 'Jesus' as merely a code-word for this.[2] Yet although they have emanated from such respectable scholars, claims like these really have little more worth than more recent ones of the genre that God was an astronaut, or Jesus was a breastless woman.

For even though we may not know exactly when Jesus was born (the year AD 1 was a miscalculation by the sixth-century monk Dionysius Exiguus), nor the year of his death, [3] he is in fact rather more securely documented than many a Roman emperor. The *Annals* of Tacitus, which provide much of our available information on the Roman emperors of Jesus's century, are known only from a single manuscript that dates from as late as the fourteenth century. We have to accept on trust that this was copied from a much earlier original. By contrast there are several hundred full texts of the gospels dating from before AD 1000, eighty fragmentary ones dating from before AD 400 (all showing reassuring consistencies with the 'received' versions), and one fragment, from John's gospel, that according to experts in the history of handwriting can be reliably dated to within a hundred years of Jesus's death. This is the so-called Rylands papyrus found in Egypt and preserved in Manchester University's John Rylands Library (Figure 1 overleaf).

Although it is smaller than a playing card, Princeton University manuscript specialist Bruce Metzger has remarked of this:

> Although the extent of the verses preserved is so slight, in one respect this tiny scrap of papyrus possesses as much evidential value as would the complete codex. As Robinson Crusoe, seeing but a single footprint in the sand, concluded that another human being, with two feet, was present on the island with him, so $\mathfrak{p}^{52}$ [the Rylands fragment's international code name] proves the existence and use of the Fourth Gospel in a little provincial town along the Nile far from its traditional place of composition (Ephesus in Asia Minor), during the first half of the second century. [4]

But yet more important than the sheer profusion and antiquity of documentation is the fact that such an individual, consistent, and striking personality emerges from the pages of the four gospels, despite their differing authorship. If there had not been a real-life Jesus of Nazareth that sparked off all this, we should have to look for someone else, equally remarkable.

One man who gave this a great deal of thought was the hard-headed New Testament Theology Professor Paul Wilhelm Schmiedel, who flourished at the University of Zürich in the first quarter of the twentieth century. Schmiedel pointed out that there are nine crucial passages in the gospels, such as Mark 3:21 (in which Jesus's family think him mad and try to take charge of him), which are simply so impossible to believe as being inventions of the early Church that for him at least there must have been a historical

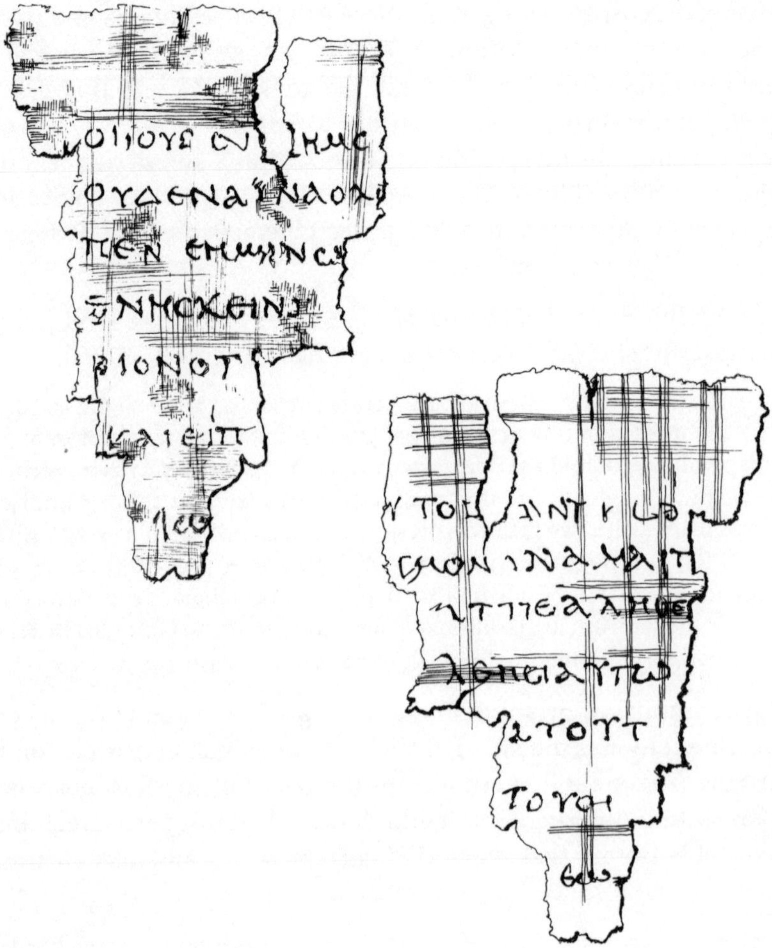

Figure 1. The earliest-known fragment from a Christian gospel, as preserved in the John Rylands Library, Manchester University. The text on the front side (left) can be identified to John 18:31–34, the back (right) to John 18:37–8. This has enabled scholars to reconstruct that the original document must have comprised a 130-page papyrus book. Stylistic features of the handwriting indicate it was written within a century of Jesus's death.

Jesus. [5]

And indeed, in this very vein, there is a lot else in the gospels which, while again arguably presenting him as mad in any normal worldly terms, reiterates Jesus's uniqueness as a historical character. Consider for instance the extremes of the conduct Jesus apparently asked of those who contemplated following him:

> Offer the wicked man no resistance ... If anyone hits you on the right cheek, offer him the other as well; if a man takes you to law and would have your tunic, let him have your cloak as well.
>
> (Matthew 5:39–41)

> Love your enemies.
>
> (Matthew 5:44)

> Leave the dead to bury their dead.
>
> (Luke 9:60)

> Sell all you own and distribute your money to the poor.
>
> (Luke 18:22)

> Happy are you when people hate you, drive you out, abuse you, denounce your name as criminal ... for then your reward will be great in heaven.
>
> (Luke 6:22–3)

> If any man comes to me without hating his father, mother, wife, children, brothers, sisters, yes, and his own life too, he cannot be my disciple.
>
> (Luke 14:25–6)

In Mark 11:14 Jesus is described as cursing a fig tree simply because it did not happen to bear fruit when he wanted it. And in Luke 9:61 he goes to the lengths of rebuking one would-be follower because he wanted to make a kind, caring gesture of going back home to say goodbye to his family. Who else has ever before or since been quite as ruthlessly radical in his promulgation of a religion of love?

And yet, in contrast to his contemporary John the Baptist, Jesus was no extremist-minded, pleasure-shunning ascetic. One of the most common settings for him in the canonical gospels, both before the Crucifixion, and in his Resurrection appearances, is that of a meal, and he appears to have been quite unabashed about enjoyment of this kind. In his own words:

> ... John the Baptist comes, not eating bread, not drinking wine, and you say, 'He is possessed'. The Son of Man comes, eating and drinking, and you say, 'Look, a glutton and a drunkard, a friend of tax collectors and sinners'.
>
> (Luke 7:33,34)

In the very next episode in Luke's gospel he is portrayed as dining in some luxury in the house of a clearly wealthy Pharisee, on this same occasion allowing a woman of apparently easy virtue to kiss and perfume his feet (Luke 7:34–50). Here was nothing if not a character.

And whatever our view of Jesus as a theological entity, a lot of other highly individual characteristics of him come tumbling into view once we focus even a modicum of interest on the sort of mind that must have been behind the canonical gospel sayings accredited to him.

One such characteristic, for instance, evident from so many of his sayings, is an extraordinary inventiveness of imagery and expression that had the added bonus, intended or otherwise, of being timeless. Consider the pictures raised in the mind by the following:

> It is easier for a camel to pass through the eye of a needle than for a rich man to enter the kingdom of God.
>
> (Mark 10:24)

> Why do you observe the splinter in your brother's eye, and never notice the plank in your own?
>
> (Matthew 7:3)

> Do not throw your pearls in front of pigs.
>
> (Matthew 7:6)

> I am sending you out like lambs among wolves.
>
> (Luke 10:3)

The opposite side of the coin to this, as pointed out by the Cambridge Ancient History professor T.R. Glover,[6] is that Jesus virtually never ever spoke in abstracts. While today our language is full of words ending in *-ity* and *-ation* that had plenty of equivalents in Jesus's time, he always avoided these in favour of words that were simple and direct.

Another of Jesus's characteristics, particularly evident in his parables, is a highly developed power of observation. The individuals with whom the parables are peopled – the unscrupulous judge, the importunate widow, the crafty steward, the virtuous Pharisee, the good Samaritan, and many more – are ones most unlikely to have sprung either from any gospel-writing by committee, or from any world-shunning mystical imagination.

It is true that parables as a Jewish literary form were already over a thousand years old even in Jesus's time. But those of Jesus had such a profound impact then, even as they do now, because they were so self-evidently based on real-life observation. This can be demonstrated not least from some of the manuscript scraps that turn up from time to time in the course of archaeological excavations, revealing glimpses of ordinary everyday life in Jesus's times.

Thus in the British Museum there is a lease-contract[7] for a vineyard that dates from 22 to 21 BC and was found in western Iran (Figure 2 - see overleaf). Witnessed by three persons, and written in duplicate, it is essentially just the sort of document that would have been drawn up for the vineyard tenant-farmers whom Jesus portrayed in his Parable of the Wicked Husbandmen (Mark 12:1–9; Matthew 21:33–41; Luke 20:9–16). Clearly Jesus had more than a nodding acquaintance with such transactions.

Similarly a second-century papyrus from the Fayum, a letter written in Greek by one Antonius Longus to his seemingly widowed mother Nilus, reveals a classic Prodigal Son scenario:

> Antonis [*sic* – an abbreviation] Longus to Nilus his mother, many greetings. And continually do I pray you are in health ... I was ashamed to come to Caranis [presumably the writer's home village] because I walk about in rags. I write to you that I am naked. I implore you, mother, be reconciled to me. Furthermore I know

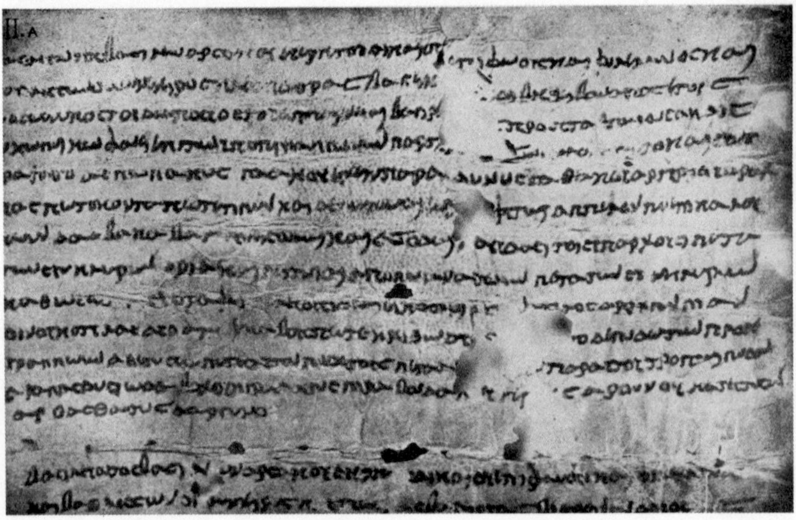

Figure 2. Contract for hereditary lease of a vineyard – a parchment found at Kopanis, Iran, part of the Parthian empire in Jesus's time, and dating from 22–21 BC. The parchment is now in the British Museum.

> what I have brought upon myself. I have been punished just as I deserve. I know that I have sinned ... [8]

Another of Jesus's self-evident characteristics deserving of mention is his clear affinity to the life of a countryman, rather than to that of a city-dweller. Among the unmistakable indications of this are the very strong elements of rural imagery and analogies to rural life that are to be found among his canonical gospel sayings. While the gospels contain absolutely no mention of Jesus having anything to do with the large Galilean town of Sepphoris, despite this being merely four miles from Nazareth, yet, even in just the thirteenth chapter of Luke's gospel, Jesus reveals himself as knowing how to revive a barren fig tree (vv. 6–9); sensitive to farm animals' need for watering (v.15); aware of the astonishing growth properties of mustard seed (v.19); conversant with the amount of yeast needed to leaven dough (v.21); and observant of how a hen 'gathers her brood under her wings' (v.34). Similar is the following from Matthew's gospel:

> Beware of false prophets who come to you disguised as sheep but underneath are ravenous wolves. You will be able to tell them by their fruits. Can people pick grapes from thorns, or figs from thistles? In the same way, a sound tree produces good fruit but a rotten tree bad fruit. A sound tree cannot bear bad fruit, nor a rotten tree bear good fruit. Any tree that does not produce good fruit is cut down and thrown on the fire.
>
> (Matthew 7:15–19)

This marked countryman affinity helps us to reconstruct another aspect of Jesus: how his very voice would have sounded to the sophisticated citizens of Jerusalem, in whose Temple he preached during the last week of his life, and in whose midst he was executed. Since Jesus's Galilee was a major agricultural region, we should perhaps not be surprised that the accent of its people carried connotations of rustic ignorance to urban-minded southerners such as the Jerusalemites. The Jewish scholar Geza Vermes is fond of quoting a story from the Talmud, the Jewish equivalent of the New Testament, featuring a Galilean being ridiculed in the Jerusalem market-place because of the sloppiness of his speech when he was trying to buy what he called *amar*. As he was told:

> 'You stupid Galilean, do you want something to ride on (*hamar*: a donkey)? Or something to drink (*hamár* : wine)? Or something for clothing (*amar* : wool)? Or something for a sacrifice (*immar* : a lamb)?'. [9]

Almost inevitably Jesus must have sounded something like this. And that his fellow Galileans certainly did is quite evident from the Matthew gospel's story of the bystanders' challenge to Peter as he waited in the high priest's courtyard while Jesus was being tried: 'You are one of them for sure! Why, your accent gives you away' (Matthew 26:73).

But it is also clear that in Jesus's case any rustic earthiness, instead of diminishing his appeal to his contemporaries, may well have given it extra edge, in a manner not dissimilar (despite the difference of personalities) to the impact of the peasant Rasputin on the court of pre-revolutionary Russia. The gospels repeatedly attest that Jesus attracted crowds of a frenzy associated today mainly with pop stars. Mark in his very first chapter noted:

> The whole town came crowding round the door.
>
> (Mark 1:32)

followed a few verses later by:

> Jesus could no longer go openly into any town, but had to stay outside in places where nobody lived. Even so, people from all around would come to him.
>
> (Mark 1:45)

By Chapter 3 we are told that at Jesus's home:

> Such a crowd collected that they could not even have a meal.
>
> (Mark 3:20)

Nor was this peculiar just to Galilee. Of Jesus's time in Jerusalem Luke recorded:

> The people as a whole hung on his words.
>
> (Luke 19:48)

and

> From early morning the people would gather round in the Temple to listen to him.
>
> (Luke 21:38)

So in order to understand more of the personality behind the gospel words, we also need to try to identify the sort of features which gave him this universal, crowd-pulling appeal.

In this regard, it is difficult for us to appreciate at the distance of two thousand years just how revolutionary was the actual message, the Good News, that both he and John the Baptist proclaimed: that because the kingdom of God was at hand (not least, by the very presence of Jesus on earth) no longer did sinners have to seek their expiation by the traditional means of the expensive monopoly operated by the Sadducean priesthood at the Jerusalem Temple. The old way was for sinners to have to travel to the Temple, from whatever part of the world they were living, there to offer sacrifice which in turn required various cash-transactions from which the Temple priests reaped suitably comfortable rake-offs.

As taught by John and Jesus, this old way had become corrupt: hence John's refuge in the wilderness, and Jesus's most violent, and ultimately fatal act of forcibly expelling the moneychangers from the Temple. John had taught that absolution could be obtained simply by true repentance, accompanied by symbolic immersion in cleansing water. Jesus, although he did not repudiate the value of baptism (for his followers would go on to make this the central rite for admission into his Church), taught, and encouraged his disciples to teach, that forgiveness could be obtained by true repentance, along with acceptance of his Word as imparted either directly, or via a disciple.

All this could never have had sway with such large numbers of people were it not accompanied by another key characteristic of Jesus, one repeatedly attested to by gospel writers: the absolute authority, the absolute conviction with which he spoke.

Early in his gospel Mark reported:

> His teaching made a deep impression on them because, unlike the scribes, he taught them with authority.
>
> (Mark 1:22)

All three synoptic gospel writers, in each case very shortly before their versions of the parable of the wicked husbandmen (whom Jesus equated with the chief priests), represented Jesus being questioned by chief priests and scribes with the words:

> What authority have you for acting like this? Or who is it that gave you this authority?
>
> (Matthew 21:23; Mark 11:28; Luke 20:2)

In fact, we do not even need the gospel writers to convey this point to us; it is quite evident from virtually every saying attributed to

Jesus, and even more so from what he did not say. Unlike theologians and churchmen of either his time or our own, it was rare in the extreme for Jesus ever to seek support from any passage in the scriptures. Unlike politicians and lawyers of either then or now, he never appealed to historical precedent. Instead, while giving analogies to illumine the justice of his remarks, he spoke straight from total conviction, total authority.

This is evident from the way he ruled on every issue brought before him: on the tribute money: 'Give to Caesar what belongs to Caesar, and to God what belongs to God,' (Luke 20:25); on the adulterous woman 'Go away, and don't sin any more,' (John 8:11); on the rich man's path to salvation: 'Sell all you own and distribute the money to the poor,' (Luke 18:22). It is equally evident from the words he is represented as using to effect his miracle cures: 'Be cured!' (Mark 1:41); 'Be quiet! Come out of him !' (Mark 1:26); 'Be opened' (Mark 8:34); 'Little girl, I tell you to get up!' (Mark 5:41). In the case of the latter these sharp, staccato commands were clearly so memorable that Mark as a gospel writer (arguably genuinely because of having heard them from Peter) actually went to the lengths of quoting them in their original Aramaic.

And in noting that the gospels preserve some of Jesus's original Aramaic, we touch on yet another aspect crucial to our understanding of him, that Aramaic was of course the language in which his words were delivered. Among Jews throughout the Roman world Aramaic had long supplanted the affiliated Hebrew, the latter having become reserved for religious usage, just as the Roman Catholic Church retained Latin. This is not to say that Jesus and his associates may not also have had some quite reasonable fluency in Greek, which was the universal language of the Roman Empire at that time. But as is quite clear from the Aramaic names of Jesus's companions (Cephas, Martha, Toma [Thomas], and those beginning with 'Bar' - 'son of'), and also those Aramaic words directly recorded of Jesus, such as *Abba* (father) in Mark 14:36, and the above mentioned 'cure' commands), Aramaic was the language in which Jesus taught, delivered his parables, carried out his cures, and conversed with all those closest to him.

The importance of this becomes clear when we learn of an intriguing discovery made by scholars who, interested in recapturing the exact words that Jesus might have used, tried translating the Greek of these as in the received gospels back into the hypothesised original Aramaic. To their astonishment, some of the sayings suddenly became poetic. For instance, in Luke's equivalent of the Sermon on the Mount Jesus is represented as saying, 'Love your enemies, do good to those who hate you, bless those who curse you, pray for those who treat you badly' (Luke 6:27–8). As pointed out by Cambridge theological scholar Don Cupitt,[10] when this is translated into Aramaic, not only does it turn into verse, it also has a characteristically Hebrew/Aramaic parallelism, the second couplet exactly echoing the first, but carrying the thought just a little further, as is evident even from the English.

Thus just as we hear in Psalm 25:

> Lord, make your ways known to me,
> Teach me your paths.
> Set me in the way of your truth, and teach me,
> For you are the God who saves me.

so Jesus says in Luke:

> Love your enemies,
> Do good to those who hate you.
> Bless those who curse you,
> Pray for those who treat you badly.
>
> (Luke 6:27-8)

There are many other examples of this verse-form, indicating that Jesus must quite deliberately have set important elements of his teaching into poetry. Arguably this was to make it more memorable, just as for much more mundane purposes we have all learnt 'Thirty days hath September ...' and 'I before e, except after c'.

So far all that we have built up as a working picture of Jesus's personality and the way he spoke has been based on the three so-called synoptic gospels of Matthew, Mark and Luke. But inevitably there is one other gospel, that of John, which must be taken into account in order to obtain an overall picture. As theological scholars have long recognised, John's gospel raises many complications because of its marked differences from the synoptics, both in the manner and the content of the speeches attributed to Jesus. In John, no longer does Jesus speak in parables. We do not find the familiar plethora of short, pithy sayings. We do not find him reproving people for acclaiming him as Christ.

Instead the Jesus of John indulges in lengthy discourses on the divinity speaking within him, urging his listeners that the only salvation lies in belief in him:

> You are from below
> I am from above.
> You are of this world
> I am not of this world.
> I have told you already: You will die in your sins
> Yes, if you do not believe that I am He,
> you will die in your sins.

(John 8:23–4)

He is quite explicit about his differentness from ordinary mortal men:

> I shall remain with you for only a short time now
> then I shall go back to the one who sent me.
> You will look for me and will not find me.
> Where I am,
> you cannot come.

(John 7:33–4)

Many nineteenth-century theologians, particularly those in Germany, felt that John presented such a different picture of Jesus that this could not be authentic. They postulated that the gospel was most likely written nearly two centuries after Jesus's lifetime, probably under the influence of the increased deification that many Christians had attributed to Jesus by this time.

Today this extreme view is no longer sustained. The already-mentioned Rylands papyrus, for instance, shows that not only had John's gospel been written by the early second century AD, copies of it had already spread well into Egypt by this time, arguably hundreds of miles from where the original manuscript was first composed. Archaeological and other discoveries have shown that John's narrative of Jesus's Passion and Crucifixion has much accurate topographical detail and convincing eye-witness description, more so than any other gospel. And for all their differences, many of Jesus's speeches in John's gospel still exhibit the characteristic rural imagery already familiar from the synoptics:

> I tell you most solemnly
> I am the gate of the sheepfold.
> All others who have come
> are thieves and brigands;
> but the sheep took no notice of them.
>
> (John 10:7–8)

> I tell you most solemnly
> unless a wheat grain falls on the ground and dies,
> it remains only a single grain;
> but if it dies
> it yields a rich harvest.
>
> (John 12:24)

As already remarked, even in the tradition of the Church John's was the last of the canonical gospels to be written, and in this regard there are indications that part of his intention was to correct his predecessors in some details. For instance, he differs from them over the length of Jesus's ministry, the timing of the expulsion of the money changers, the day of the week of the Last Supper, and of the Crucifixion. Arguably, if he was indeed one and the same as the 'beloved disciple' of John 13:23, he may have been better informed than the synoptic writers.

But was the other, far greater part of John's intention to set down the more 'hidden' side to Jesus's teaching – a gospel with Jesus's most explicit explanations of his real nature and purpose, which had not been spoken openly, and which he could only give in private to his most immediate and trusted followers? Even in the synoptic gospels there are hints that there genuinely was such a hidden side to Jesus's teaching, as in Mark's:

> The secret of the kingdom of God is given to you, but to those who are outside everything comes in parables.
>
> (Mark 4:11)

and Matthew's:

> Everything that is now covered will be uncovered, and everything now hidden will be made clear. What I say to you in the dark, tell in the daylight.
>
> (Matthew 10:26–7)

As we will see in later chapters, a great deal of the non-canonical material attributed to Jesus, authentic or otherwise, consists of material of this genre. And as we shall also see, determining the exact criteria of authenticity for all material, even that already within the canonical gospels, can, in some instances, present even greater difficulties than might be commonly supposed....

Chapter 3

Quest for the Authentic

In the quest for what might be authentic words of Jesus, it is important to guard against any too facile judgments. For instance a single manuscript of the eighteenth century purporting to have been copied from a lost gospel of the first or second century might appear to have a very slim claim to reproduce authentic words of Jesus. Yet, as has already been pointed out, we have very little better than this in the case of the manuscript which has given us works of Tacitus. However, in the Tacitus example it would take a brave scholar indeed to cry fraud. This is quite simply because the content itself carries such a strong ring of authenticity. Later in this book we will come across a reputedly 'lost gospel' example of precisely this kind.

Hypothetically, the other end of the extreme would be a piece of papyrus carrying the words 'Jesus said', followed by a saying otherwise unknown either from the canonical gospels or from any other source. Let us suppose that radiocarbon dating and handwriting analysis mutually supported each other that this scrap must have been written within a century of Jesus's lifetime, just as we have seen of the Rylands papyrus. Yet even such unimpeachable antiquity is on its own no more certain a criterion of authenticity than a claim that Michelangelo must have painted the *Mona Lisa*, simply because he lived at the right time and in the right city. Content is crucial, with serious questions to be raised if there is anything about the saying that has a suspect or unfamiliar ring.

In this regard, demanding of the greatest caution and vigilance are any signs of the heretical early Christian movement known as Gnosticism. According to the eighteenth-century historian Edward Gibbon, the Gnostics were 'distinguished as the most polite, the most learned, and the most wealthy of the Christian name', yet despite this, Gnostic works were highest on the list of those non-canonical gospels which the fifth-century *Decretum Gelasianum* condemned as apocryphal.

Having its root in mystical ideas that had first formed in pagan circles, Christian Gnosticism took a variety of forms, from the Valentinian, which had its inspiration in the dualist teachings of the Egyptian Valentinus, to the Marcionite, as founded by the law-confounding, love-inspired Marcion.[1] But while such schools differed in various ways one from another, they all shared common ground in the idea of the overwhelming importance of Gnosis, or inner knowledge. Fired by belief in the workings of this from within, it was all too easy for the Gnostic of centuries after Jesus's lifetime to write in all sincerity a gospel of what he (or she) thought Jesus might have said, without this bearing the slightest relation to anything that might genuinely have come from the flesh and blood Jesus of history. Later in this book we will encounter examples of just this kind.

Yet complicating all this is that there is no easy dividing line between at least some of this sort of Gnosticism and the sort of hidden teaching which we have just noted to be the chief characteristic of the canonical gospel of John. Clearly our only recourse is to take each purported saying on its merits, to take into account every facet of background information that we may have, and to be ever-watchful for surprises from any quarter. As we are about to discover, these can even come from within the canonical gospels themselves.

For while it might be thought that the last place for us to look for any non-canonical sayings of Jesus would be actually within the canonical gospels, in fact this is precisely the case with one most well-known episode from the gospels, the episode in question being none other than the famous incident of Jesus and the woman who had committed adultery, with which we began this book. Before the reader begins to wonder how such an apparently canonical passage can possibly have come from a non-canonical source, let me first quote the passage in full, so that we can refresh our memories of its content:

> They all went home, and Jesus went to the Mount of Olives. At daybreak he appeared in the Temple again; and as all the people came to him, he sat down and began to teach them. The scribes and Pharisees brought a woman along who had been caught committing adultery; and making her stand there in full view of everybody they said to Jesus, 'Master, this woman was caught in the very act of committing adultery, and Moses has ordered us in the Law to condemn women like this to death by stoning. What do you have to say?'. They asked him this as a test, looking for something to use against him. But Jesus bent down and started writing on the ground with his finger. As they persisted with their question, he looked up and said, 'If there is one of you who has not sinned, let him be the first to throw a stone at her'. Then he bent down and wrote on the ground again. When they heard this they went away one by one, beginning with the eldest, until Jesus was left alone with the woman, who remained standing there. He looked up and said, 'Woman, where are they? Has no-one condemned you?'. 'No-one, sir,' she replied. 'Neither do I condemn you,' said Jesus, 'Go away, and don't sin any more'.
>
> (John 7:53 to 8:11)

Now, as noted, this passage appears in our present-day Bibles as part of John's gospel, and most ordinary present-day Christians quite understandably assume that that is where it must always have belonged. This is despite the fact that the passage, although it has no counterpart in the synoptic gospels, seems out of tune with the long speeches and similar characteristics of John's gospel, and sounds as if it ought to have come from one of the synoptics.

The plot thickens when we return to the early Middle Ages, and check whether the passage appeared in most Christian Bibles then. The answer is an emphatic 'no'. When in the nineteenth century the great German scholar Constantin Tischendorf discovered at St Catherine's monastery, Sinai, the famous *Codex Sinaiticus*, dating from the fourth century AD, and comprising one of the earliest-known complete texts of the gospels, he did not fail to notice that the adulterous woman story was not at its seemingly appointed place in John's gospel, nor was it anywhere else to be found. It is similarly missing from Rome's *Codex Vaticanus*, which dates from the fifth century. The earliest Greek commentator to mention the passage was Byzantine theologian Euthymius Zigabenus, writing around AD 1118. The so-called Ferrar group of New Testament manuscripts, written in Calabria between the eleventh and thirteenth centuries, set the passage to follow Luke Chapter 21 verse 38. As is well accepted by modern scholars, it quite simply was never part of the original John gospel, nor did it belong to Luke either. [2]

So how has it appeared in our Bibles, and why has it apparently so readily been accepted as authentic? The reason for this lies in a single fifth-century manuscript of the gospels and Acts, with a text in Greek and Latin, that is today known as the *Codex Bezae*. In the middle of the sixteenth century this manuscript happened to be the one most at hand for use as a prime source for publication of the Greek so-called 'received text' of our Bible, and in 1581 it was presented to the University of Cambridge by the Calvinist theologian Theodore Beza (or De Besze) after whom it has been named. Since at that stage scholars did not know of the existence of *Sinaiticus*, and as Protestants the *Codex Vaticanus* was inaccessible to them, neither the fact nor the significance of the general omission of the adulterous woman passage was realised.

But if, as this seems to indicate, the author of the John gospel did not write the story of the adulterous woman, then the question arises of who did; or at the very least, how far back can the story be traced? That it was of sufficient antiquity to have been known at least as early as the third century is apparent from mention of it in the so-called *Didascalia Apostolorum*, a treatise on Christian codes of conduct that appears to have been written by a doctor from north Syria who had been converted to Christianity from Judaism.

The most promising clue to its origin comes from a cryptic mention early in the following century in Bishop Eusebius of Caesarea's *History of the Church.* As part of his typically copious references to early documents Eusebius remarks of the early second-century historian Papias (whose works have otherwise been lost to us), that he '... reproduces a story about a woman falsely accused before the Lord of many sins. *This is to be found in the Gospel of the Hebrews*'[3] [italics mine].

Now as will be recalled from the first chapter the 'Gospel of the Hebrews' was a lost Aramaic gospel text much favoured by Jewish Christian groups such as the Ebionites. There appears to have been nothing heretical about it, since Eusebius (who evidently had his own copy) tells us that it was used by the perfectly orthodox but Jewish-born Christian historian Hegesippus (circa second century AD).[4] Similarly the late fourth-century/early fifth-century scholar St Jerome, who was responsible for rendering the Bible into Latin, considered the 'Gospel of the Hebrews' worthwhile enough to translate it into both Latin and Greek.

Some caution is needed as to whether Eusebius's 'woman falsely accused' was really one and the same as the adulterous woman, since, rather than having been falsely accused, the latter was actually caught in the act. However, most scholars still do accept this identity.

But if the 'Gospel of the Hebrews' did indeed include the adulterous woman story, then the very fact of this passage's total convincingness as an episode in the life of Jesus, complete with its equally convincing sayings by him, raises special interest in other things, particularly what sayings of Jesus this gospel might have contained. Here we are fortunate that at least some other elements of its content have been preserved in the form of extracts quoted by early Church fathers. St Jerome, for instance, reproduced from it a story of Jesus's baptism:

> Behold the mother of the Lord and his brothers said to him, 'John is baptising for the remission of sins; let us go and be baptised by him'. But he said to them, 'What sin have I committed, that I should go and be baptised by him - unless perhaps this very statement that I have made is ignorance?'.[5]

Disappointingly, although this passage again has no equivalent in any of the canonical gospels, it is in fact rather less convincing than the adulterous woman story. Many early Christians had been puzzled by John the Baptist's well-recorded baptism of Jesus, on the grounds that if Jesus was sinless, why should he have taken part in a ritual specially designed to wash sins away? Accordingly, while the passage's authenticity is not impossible, it does sound rather too much as if it might have been written as a form of apology to allay concerns of this kind, rather than as a genuine record of what historically once happened.

Much more credible, on the other hand, is another fragment from the gospel preserved by Jerome, comprising the apparent saying by Jesus:

> For the prophets also, even after having been anointed by the Holy Spirit, could be sinful in what they spoke.[6]

Early this century the eminent Cambridge Professor of Divinity Dr F.C. Burkitt adjudged this one most likely to be authentic on the grounds that only someone of Jesus's calibre would have dared be so critical of anointed Jewish prophets, particularly bearing in mind that the gospel in which it appears was one used by Jewish-born followers.

Jerome and other early fathers also quote from the 'Gospel of the Hebrews' some additional isolated sayings of Jesus that are of more than passing interest:

> Never be glad, except when you look upon your brother with love.[7]
>
> I choose for myself the best that my Father who is in heaven gives me.[8]
>
> He who seeks will not cease until he finds; when he finds he will be astonished; when he is astonished, he will reign; when he reigns, he will rest.[9]

The first of these is a reasonably credible, but otherwise unparalleled variation on Jesus's fundamental theme of love for fellow humanity. The second seems to be an alternative form of part of Jesus's prayer to God as given in chapter 17 of John's gospel:

> I have made your name known to the men you took from the world to give me.
>
> (John 17:6)

The third, which is much more obscure, seems at least related to the words of Matthew 7:7 and Luke 11:9: 'Search and you will find; knock and the door will be opened to you'.

But perhaps the most interesting, and indeed astonishing surviving extract from the 'Gospel of the Hebrews', and it is one which again we owe to St Jerome, is a completely unparalleled description of a purported post-Resurrection appearance by Jesus to his brother James:

> But the Lord, when he had given the *sindon* to the high priest's servant, went to James and appeared to him. For James had sworn that he would not eat bread from that hour when he had drunk the Lord's cup until he saw him rising from those who sleep.... 'Bring,' says the Lord, 'a table and bread'. He took bread and blessed it and broke it and gave it to James the Righteous and said to him, 'My brother, eat your bread, for the Son of Man has risen from those who sleep'.[10]

Now of all the material in the canonical gospels, the stories of Jesus's Resurrection have always been the most confused and problematic. In the case of Mark's gospel, for instance, the earliest-known manuscripts end abruptly after verse 8 of the last chapter, thus omitting any description of Jesus's Resurrection appearances. There are any number of inconsistencies between one gospel and another concerning how many women went to the tomb; how many young men/angels were there to greet them; whether Jesus subsequently appeared to his disciples in Galilee (Matthew and received Mark), or Jerusalem (Luke and John); etc., etc. Accordingly, any light thrown even by a non-canonical gospel has to be considered valuable.

Here, adding considerable credence to the 'Gospel of the Hebrews' assertion that Jesus appeared to James after his Resurrection, is the fact that Paul quite independently states exactly this in his first letter to the Corinthians:

> ... he appeared first to Cephas [Simon Peter] and secondly to the Twelve. Next he appeared to more than five hundred of the brothers at the same time, most of whom are still alive, though some have died; *then he appeared to James* [italics mine], and then to all the apostles.
>
> (I Corinthians 15: 5–7)

The question that has to be immediately raised is why there should be no mention of such an important-sounding appearance in any of the canonical gospels. It becomes even more intriguing when we realise that this is not the only mystery relating to James, Jesus's brother. Although James is accorded but the most glancing mention in the canonical gospels, specifically the passage in Mark:

> This is the carpenter, surely, the son of Mary, the brother of James and Joset and Jude and Simon. His sisters too, are they not here with us?
>
> (Mark 6:3)

– in Acts he appears as the head of the Jerusalem Church, the very earliest community of Jesus's followers, commanding apparent authority to 'rule' over the apostle Simon Peter on the matter of Gentile Christians being allowed to be circumcised. That this James, brother of Jesus, so neglected by the canonical gospels, actually had such eminence in the immediate wake of his brother's death is corroborated by a passage from the second-century Jewish Christian historian Hegesippus:

> Control of the Church passed to the apostles, together with the Lord's brother James, whom everyone from the Lord's time till our own has called the Righteous .... [11]

and one from Clement of Alexandria, who wrote in Book 6 of his *Outlines*:

> Peter, James [the Apostle] and John, after the Ascension of the Saviour, did not claim pre-eminence ... but chose James the Righteous as Bishop of Jerusalem. [12]

Now inevitably Christians laying great store by the Virgin Mary cult are often somewhat troubled by gospel references to Jesus's brothers and sisters, sometimes trying to explain them away, somewhat unconvincingly, as cousins, even though the Greek of Luke's gospel quite explicitly describes Jesus as Mary's 'first-born' (Luke 2:7). Yet whatever the exact relationship, James seems most likely to have been one of those relatives who, when Jesus created chaos in his household because of the crowds who came to hear him and be taught by him, 'set out to take charge of him, convinced he was out of his mind' (Mark 3:32).

Furthermore the canonical gospels only thinly disguise that Jesus seems to have been at odds with his family right up to the time of his Crucifixion. That even when Jesus was hanging on the cross neither James nor any other brother was around seems to be quite apparent from the John gospel's information that it was on the 'beloved disciple' (as earlier remarked, generally thought to have been John the Evangelist himself), that Jesus bestowed the care of his mother (John 19:26–7).

Yet as we learn from the book of Acts, just forty days later, following the very time in which Jesus had been making the Resurrection appearances that included the one to James, those same brothers together with his mother joined the apostles in the Jerusalem upstairs room in which they all met in the immediate aftermath of the Ascension. From this point on, as if there had been no earlier problem, James seems by common consent to have become head of that first Jerusalem Christian community who, as described in Acts, 'lived together and owned everything in common', and 'went as a body to the Temple every day but met in their houses for the breaking of bread' (Acts 2:45–6).

So what could have happened in such a short time to transform James so radically from one apparently outside Jesus's immediate circle of followers, to his dead brother's number one earthly representative? Could it have been the shock and certainty created by the very Resurrection appearance which we have glimpsed so tantalisingly in Jerome's extract from the 'Gospel of the Hebrews'?

In this regard, there are endless curiosities to the 'Hebrews' passage. It implies, for instance, that James had been present at the Last Supper, as suggested by the reference to 'that hour when he had drunk the Lord's cup'.

But if so, why did the canonical authors again omit any mention of this, particularly when James seems to have taken a somewhat rash oath not to eat bread until his brother's Resurrection? What is the explanation of Jesus seemingly first having appeared to the 'high priest's servant'? Was this the Malchus whose ear was cut off by Peter in Gethsemane (John 18:10)? And whoever this man was, why did Jesus give him his *sindon*, a word deliberately left untranslated (because it simply means linen cloth), but which it is difficult to interpret as other than the shroud which the synoptic writers describe as used to wrap Jesus's body for burial?

Almost certainly none of these questions can be properly resolved unless there happens one day to be discovered a full text of 'Gospel of the Hebrews', a discovery which, were it to happen, could create far more reverberations than even the Dead Sea Scrolls.

But arguably whoever did write the 'Gospel of the Hebrews' knew and recorded rather more information than has been preserved in the canonical gospels. He also had some otherwise unique insights into the still all too mysterious circumstances surrounding Jesus's Resurrection. And among several indications that the 'Hebrews' writer would have preserved other genuine sayings of Jesus is the characteristic authority which Jesus exhibits in his remarks to James, and the very convincing manner in which he is represented as using the 'Son of Man' title of himself, a trait otherwise particular to the canonical gospels, with just one exception in Acts 7:56.

It is interesting also to note that the *Codex Bezae*, in addition to the story of the adulterous woman, has as part of Luke's gospel another saying of Jesus otherwise not included in New Testament manuscripts. At Luke 6:5, in place of the normal 'and he said to them, "The Son of Man is master of the Sabbath"' *Bezae* has:

> On the same day, seeing a man working on the Sabbath, he said to him, 'If you know what you are doing, you are a happy man! But if you do not know, you are accursed and a Lawbreaker'.

As most scholars have felt, this has a distinctive touch of authenticity because, like so much of what Jesus said, it is subtle and contains the element of the unexpected. Of the man working on the Sabbath it seems to be saying that if he had considered his transgression of the Jewish Law carefully, and had honestly squared it with his conscience, then he was doing no wrong. It was as if he did not care that he deserved the Law's full condemnation. How such passages crept into the *Codex Bezae* remains of course a mystery. Did some early scribe, knowing that only the gospels of Matthew, Mark, Luke and John had been chosen for preservation as Holy Writ, decide to slip these into the text he was copying, as a means of preserving them? If this was the case, it can only cause us to wonder what other gems of Jesus's life remain still lost.

But what of any of the early other non-canonical gospels? As remarked earlier, the 'Gospel of the Egyptians' was another of the non-canonical gospels of which occasional quotations have been preserved by early Church fathers. This gospel, which is thought to have been written in Egypt in the first half of the second century, was certainly known to the second-century theologian Clement of Alexandria, to the Gnostic Theodotus, and to the third-century Alexandrian Biblical critic Origen, and all of them have left some brief references to it.

One of the most substantial extracts of this kind comes from Clement of Alexandria, and takes the form of a conversation between Jesus and a woman called Salome, possibly the same as the Salome described as among the women who watched Jesus's Crucifixion 'from a distance' in Mark 15:40. From Clement's comments the text of this particular episode can be roughly reconstructed as follows:

> Salome said, 'How long will men die?'.
>
> The Lord replies, 'As long as you women have children'.
>
> Salome replied, 'I did well, then, by not having children'.
>
> The Lord said, 'Eat every plant, but do not eat the one which contains bitterness'.

> Salome asked when what she was inquiring about would be known.
>
> The Lord said, 'When you trample on the garment of shame, and when the two become one, and the male with the female neither male nor female'.[13]

Clement also quotes from the same gospel another text which sounds positively anti-feminist:

> The Saviour himself said, 'I came to destroy the works of the female'.[14]

Here, as is immediately obvious, these references have virtually nothing of the 'feel' of authenticity to them that was so promising in respect of the 'Hebrews' gospel. So have we here come across a first example of the sort of spuriousness we warned ourselves to expect from the works of Gnosticism? Indeed, this seems to be the case. The first has a typically Gnostic air of the arcane, while the second exhibits a misogyny quite uncharacteristic of the Jesus of the canonical gospels. It is quite apparent from the latter that Jesus attracted a large retinue of women, e.g:

> With him went the twelve, as well as certain women who had been cured of evil spirits and ailments: Mary, surnamed the Magdalen, from whom seven demons had gone out, Joanna the wife of Herod's steward Chuza, Susanna and several others who provided for them out of their own resources.
>
> (Luke 8:1–3)

There are also several canonically reported instances of Jesus surprising his disciples by going out of his way to talk to a woman at considerable length, as in John 4:27: 'The disciples returned and were surprised to find him speaking to a woman', and in Luke 10:38-42, in which he becomes so involved in a lengthy discourse with Mary of Bethany that even her sister Martha thinks he has gone too far. Emphasis on male superiority, and exclusivity towards the male sex, were typical of some of the pagan mystery religions in which Gnosticism had its roots, and we may therefore confidently reject as not genuine sayings of Jesus at least these extracts from the 'Gospel of the Egyptians'.

But as we are about to see, not all purported sayings emanating from Egypt are to be rejected so easily. Some of the most important material for our study has been retrieved quite literally from that country's dust....

Chapter 4

Words from the Dust

On the east bank of the Nile a little to the north of Luxor in Upper Egypt lies Akhmim, a town once studded with temples during ancient Egypt's heyday, but today largely robbed of even the stone of those ancient buildings. In the winter of 1886-87 a French archaeological team was excavating the graves of a later Christian community on the site when they happened to unearth a small, bound manuscript consisting of thirty-three parchment pages covered with Greek writing. The date of the actual manuscript was comparatively late, of the eighth or ninth century, but its contents were a revelation, for they included part of a substantially earlier non-canonical gospel, the 'Gospel of Peter'. Although the existence of this gospel was known and referred to by Church fathers from as early as the second century AD, up until the French team's discovery nothing of its contents was known to have survived. [1]

In the event the discovery proved a disappointment. As had been duly noted in Bishop Eusebius's *History of the Church*, the theologian Bishop Serapion of Antioch around AD 190 wrote a highly critical pamphlet, *The So-called Gospel of Peter*, roundly condemning this gospel as false. According to the extract from Serapion quoted by Eusebius:

> We, my brothers, receive Peter and all the apostles as we receive Christ, but the writings falsely attributed to them we are experienced enough to reject, knowing that nothing of the sort has been handed down to us. [2]

As Serapion made clear, while much of the gospel 'accorded with the authentic teaching of the Saviour' it did not have the apostolic authorship claimed of it, and had been adulterated with ideas of the Docetic heresy, which suggested that as Jesus was divine, he merely appeared to go through the sufferings of crucifixion.

When the discovered manuscript was translated from its original Greek, Serapion's comments proved fully justified. Consisting predominantly of the events of Jesus's Crucifixion, the gospel broadly conveys the same sequence of events, but refers to Jesus, in contrast with the robbers crucified with him, as being silent while nailed to the cross 'since he felt no pain'. It also adds some rather palpably apocryphal details to the events of Jesus's Resurrection.

Of any actual sayings of Jesus, apart from the word 'Yes', it offers only one, Jesus's dying cry on the cross. And instead of Mark's rendition, 'My God, my God, why have you deserted me?' (Mark 15:34), for which Mark had been careful to quote Jesus's apparent exact Aramaic words, the 'Peter' writer substitutes, 'My power, my power, you have deserted me?' suggesting a corruption or, at best, mis-translation. The 'Gospel of Peter' must therefore be adjudged as adding nothing whatsoever to our knowledge of the sayings of Jesus.

Altogether more interesting, however, is another find from Egypt, even though this is in outward appearance much less impressive than the gospel from Akhmim. Known as Egerton Papyrus 2, it is preserved in the British Museum, and consists of four papyrus fragments that once belonged to three leaves from an ancient codex. Only two of the fragments are sufficiently large and intact to be decipherable, and the exact circumstances of their discovery are unknown, but the handwriting on them can be dated even at the most conservative estimate to AD 150, and quite possibly to a few decades earlier. From their content, which includes direct sayings of Jesus, they are quite clearly from a Christian gospel, thus making them almost certainly the earliest surviving Christian manuscript. But also quite evident is that although they contain some material familiar enough from the canonical gospels, they are of some unknown authorship quite independent of Matthew, Mark, Luke and John.

So far as it is possible to be deciphered, the first side of the first fragment reads:

> [?And Jesus said] to the lawyers, '[?Punish] every criminal and law-breaker, and not me;' ... And turning to the people's leaders he spoke this saying, 'You study the scriptures, believing that in them you have eternal life; these same scriptures testify to me. Do not imagine that I am going to accuse you before my Father; you place your hopes on Moses, and Moses will be your accuser.' And when they said, 'We know well that God spoke to Moses, but as for you, we do not know where you come from', Jesus answered and said to them, 'Now it is your lack of faith that is accused ...'. [3]

Overleaf, clearly after a portion that is missing, the text goes on:

> [?They urged] the crowds to [?take up] stones and stone him. And the leaders tried to lay hands on him and take him and [?hand him over] to the crowds; but they could not arrest him, because his time of betrayal had not yet come. And he slipped through the crowds. And a leper came up to him and said, 'Rabbi Jesus, through travelling with lepers and having meals with them at the inn, I too have become a leper. If you want to, you can cure me'. Jesus then said to him, 'Of course I want to! Be cured!'. And his leprosy was cured at once. [And Jesus said to him] 'Go [and show yourself] to the [priests]'.

Whether in order of pages the second fragment preceded or followed the first is unclear, as again there is too much missing. All that can be read of the first side is:

> ... coming up to him began to test him with a question, saying, 'Rabbi Jesus, we know you are from God, for the prophets testify to the things you do. Tell us, then: Is it permissible [?to pay] taxes to those who rule over us? [Should we pay them], or not?' But Jesus, reading their thoughts, said to them indignantly, 'Why do you call me Rabbi, when you don't listen to what I tell you? It was of you that Isaiah so rightly prophesied when he said, "This people honours me only with lip-service, while their hearts are far from me. The worship they offer me is worthless, [the doctrines they teach are only human] regulations ..."'.

Overleaf, the final side reads:

> enclosed ... in ... place ... its abundance immeasurable? And when they were perplexed at his strange question Jesus, as he walked, stood still on the edge of the river Jordan, and stretching out his right hand he ... and sprinkled it on the ... And then ... water that had been sprinkled ... before them and brought forth fruit ...

As will be evident to anyone familiar with the New Testament, virtually every sentence quoted here has some form of parallel in the four canonical gospels, and relates to episodes from before Jesus's arrest. For instance, in the case of the first page of the first fragment, virtually every sentence except the first has counterparts in John's gospel. In John Chapter 5 we read:

> You study the scriptures, believing that in them you have eternal life, now these same scriptures testify to me (v.39) ... Do not imagine that I am going to accuse you before the Father: you place your hopes in Moses, and Moses will be your accuser (v.45).

followed in Chapter 9 by:

> We know that God has spoken to Moses, but as for this man, we do not know where he comes from (v.29).

With regard to the reverse side, on the subject of the stone throwing, John again provides parallels, though rather less exact ones, in Chapters 7, (vv.30 and 44); 8 (v.59); and 10 (vv.31 and 39). Not so, however, the story of the healing of the leper. In this instance it is the three synoptic gospels (Matthew 8:2–3; Mark 1:40–2; and Luke 5:12–13) that have parallel passages, although these have nothing of the Egerton's account of how the leper contracted the disease.

The first side of the second fragment is relatively easily recognisable as a somewhat inferior version of the synoptic gospels' story of Jesus and the tribute money (Matthew 22:16; Mark 12:14; Luke 20:21), with the exception that the closing remark 'It was of you that Isaiah prophesied...' can be traced to Matthew 15:7–9 and Mark 7:6–7. Only the second side, which has the added disadvantage of being so incomplete, quite clearly has no canonical parallel.

We are accordingly presented with a gospel whose author appears to have had some awareness of all four canonical gospels, although he has not in fact followed their texts at all closely, and seems to have had some form of fund of his own material. There is also not the slightest indication of any heresy.

Furthermore, highly relevant to our study is that this unknown gospel includes two otherwise unknown sayings, albeit both frustratingly incomplete. The first is the opening sentence of the first fragment:

> And Jesus said to the lawyers, '[?Punish] every criminal and lawbreaker, and not me...'.

Clearly, without knowledge of the missing words and their context this is scarcely much of an addition to our knowledge of Jesus.

But a little more substantial is the passage on the reverse side of the second fragment - except for the all-important saying of Jesus, of which quite clearly a vital portion is missing. However we are at least fortunate to have been left by the New Testament scholar C.H. Dodd an interesting reconstruction of how the passage *may* have read:

> ['When a husbandman] has enclosed [a small seed] in [a hidden] place [so that it is invisibly buried, how does] its abundance [become] immeasurable?' And when they were perplexed at the strange question, then Jesus, as he walked, stood still on the edge of the river Jordan, and stretching forth his right hand, he [filled it with water] and sprinkled it upon the [shore]; and thereupon the sprinkled water [made the ground moist, and it was watered] before them, and brought forth fruit. [4]

It may not seem much - and Dodd's reconstruction is at best highly tenuous - yet even glimpsed in this imperfect state it has about it the tantalising quality of just the sort of saying and accompanying 'miracle' that we might genuinely expect from the countryman element to Jesus that we noted in Chapter 2.

That is about all this unknown gospel can offer. But it represents by no means the sum total of non-canonical sayings of Jesus to have been retrieved from the sands of Egypt. For in 1897 two young Oxford graduates, Bernard Grenfell and Arthur Hunt, sponsored by the Egypt Exploration Fund and fired specifically with the idea of finding early Christian manuscripts, began to excavate some huge ancient rubbish tips at a site called Oxyrhynchus, 120 miles to the south of Cairo. During the first centuries after Jesus's death there had been a Christian monastic settlement at Oxyrhynchus, and Grenfell and Hunt reasoned that amongst the settlement's refuse, besides other material of interest to students of ancient history, there just might lie scraps from discarded gospels.

Unlike those who searched for pharaonic tombs, the task chosen by Grenfell and Hunt was no glamorous one; in Grenfell's words:

> ... standing all day to be half choked and blinded by the peculiarly pungent dust of ancient rubbish, blended on most days with the not less irritating sand of the desert; probably drinking water which not even the East London waterworks would have ventured to supply to its consumers, and keeping incessant watch over men [their seventy-strong workforce] who, however much you may flatter yourself to the contrary, will steal if they get the chance and think it worth their while to do so. [5]

But, as they became aware, there was one type of rubbish layer, called *afsh* by the fellahin, consisting of soil mixed with straw or twigs, which was particularly promising for the preservation of papyri. And by pursuing such layers much as gold-diggers look for veins of quartz, soon not only papyrus scraps but even complete documents began to appear. Many of these were private letters, and legal documents, but there was other material in the distinctive uncial lettering characteristic of religious and literary texts. So, could there be pages from an early gospel among these?

It was Hunt, the younger, more palaeographically-inclined of the two, who soon began the task of preliminary sorting of the accumulating finds. And on only the second day of this work, as he was smoothing out a rectangular-shaped piece that seemed to have come from a numbered, paged book (Figure 3), he happened to notice on the text's second line the Greek word καρφος (karphos). From his excellent Biblical knowledge, Hunt recognised this instantly as the word translated as 'mote' in the King James version of Jesus's famous saying from Matthew's and Luke's gospels:

> And why beholdest thou the mote that is in thy brother's eye, but considerest not the beam that is in thine own eye?
>
> (Matthew 7:3-5 and Luke 6:41)

Reading the passage further, Hunt also saw that while it had to be the same saying, it was in a slightly different form: 'and then you will clearly see to cast the mote from your brother's eye'. [6]

Then he read further:

> Jesus said: 'If you do not fast from the world, you will not find the Kingdom of God, and if you do not keep the Sabbath for the whole week, you will not see the Father'.

As we have seen earlier in the case of the unknown gospel, this one had both familiar material in a slightly altered form, and new material. But instead of the fragmentary nature of the unknown gospel, this one was substantially more complete, and it seemed specifically directed to sayings of Jesus, including some of a novelty and ring of authenticity that seemed sensational. As Hunt read on:

> Jesus said, 'I stood in the midst of the world, and I appeared to them in flesh: and I found all men drunk, with no one of them thirsty. And my soul grieves for the sons of men, because their hearts are blind and they do not see...'.

To Hunt at that moment, although the saying had no exact parallel in the canonical gospels, it nonetheless sounded very convincing as the sort of utterance that might well have come from Jesus. Part of the end of the passage was missing, but turning over the page, he read:

> [Jesus said] 'Wherever there are two [they are not without] God, and wherever there is one alone I say I am with him. Raise the stone, and there you will find me. Cleave the wood, and I am there'.

Hunt marvelled at this one. He knew from Matthew's gospel the

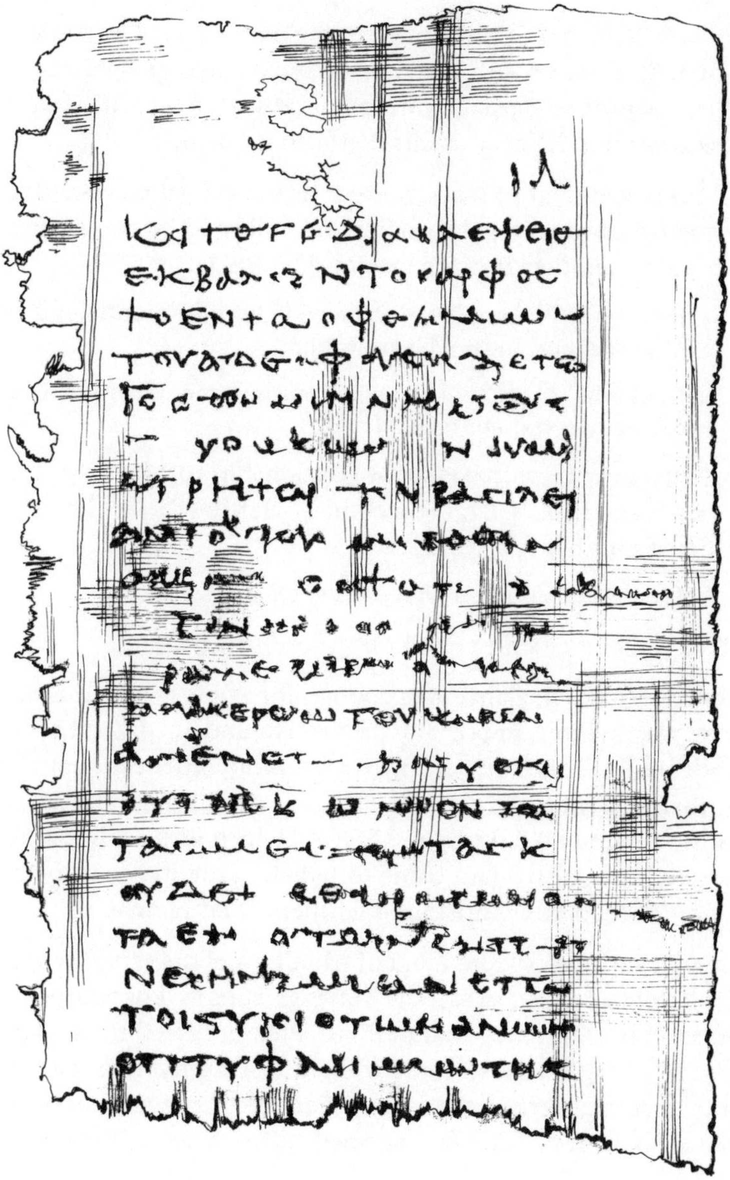

Figure 3. The papyrus fragment from Oxyrhynchus that so fascinated Oxford scholar Arthur Hunt. The word καρφος (karphos) which attracted his attention can be seen at the end of the second line.

saying 'Where two or three meet in my name, I shall be there with them' (Matthew 18:20). But this version from the gospel fragment seemed yet more special, and was to be such a lifetime source of inspiration that he even enshrined it in a poem.

Still translating, Hunt read another 'Jesus said' (this seemed to be a standard formula for the document) followed by two sayings at least partly familiar from the synoptic gospels:

> Jesus said, 'No prophet is accepted in his own country, nor can a physician heal those who know him'.
>
> Jesus said, 'A city built on the top of a high mountain and fortified can neither fall, nor be hidden'.

The first seemed to have some relationship to Matthew 13:57; Mark 6:4 and Luke 4:24; the second to Matthew 5:14. Then there were just another few words:

> Jesus said, 'You hear with one ear what ...'

before the text again petered out into disintegration.

Even such a quick glance was enough for Hunt to realise that this scrap was a most important discovery, and in the subsequent publication of hundreds of Oxyrhynchus documents he gave it the number one place. Careful scrutiny established the style of writing to date no later than AD 200, which at that time (before the unknown gospel had come to light), made it a century and a half older than any Christian document then known.

But still the mystery remained of what gospel the scrap was from. Was it from a collection of Jesus's sayings, such as those purportedly collected by Matthew, that perhaps even predated the canonical gospels? In 1903 there came to light at Oxyrhynchus two fresh scraps, seemingly from the same collection of sayings, but in much poorer condition. The first seemed to be an introduction:

> These are the [...] words which the living Jesus [...] spoke to [...] and to Thomas. And he said [whoever hears] these words shall not taste [death].

There then followed a just decipherable:

> [Jesus said] 'Let not him who seeks cease [until he] finds, and when he finds [he will be astonished]; when he is astonished, he will reign; [when he reigns], he will rest.'

To scholars of the time this second saying struck a chord outside the canonical gospels - among just those sayings of Jesus preserved by early Church fathers from non-canonical gospels that we discussed in the last chapter. Surely this was one and the same as the saying preserved by Clement of Alexandria:

> He who seeks will not cease until he finds; when he finds he will be astonished; when he is astonished, he will reign; when he reigns, he will rest. [7]

And did not Clement say that this came from the 'Gospel of the Hebrews'? For at least one prominent Biblical scholar of the time, Professor Evelyn White, who wrote a definitive account of the Oxyrhynchus sayings in 1920,[8] this seemed to point to the view that the Oxyrhynchus scraps were from the hitherto lost 'Gospel of the Hebrews', and thereby of a particularly high claim to authenticity. Other equally eminent scholars were not so sure, not least because of the persistent sayings form of the Oxyrhynchus material compared to the narrative form of some of the known content from the 'Gospel of the Hebrews'.

But no one of that time could know that the mystery was about to be most spectacularly solved by a chance discovery, made still in Egypt, but some 400 miles further to the south of Oxyrhynchus, in the year 1945.

Chapter 5

Words Preserved by Thomas?

During the month of December it is common practice for peasant farmers of the Nag Hammadi region in Upper Egypt to set off on their camels into the nearby Jabal al-Tarif mountainside in search of *sabakh*, a soft, nitrate-rich soil which they use as a natural fertiliser. Early one December day in 1945 an Arab peasant called Muhammad 'Ali al-Samman was out on just such a mission near the village of Hamra Dum when one of his brothers, digging beneath a huge boulder, came across a large earthenware jar, some three feet tall and carefully sealed. According to Muhammad 'Ali's own account,[1] he was at first frightened that the jar might contain a jinn, a bad spirit, and he was on his own when he eventually summoned the courage to smash the vessel open with his mattock. But whatever his expectations may have been, they were hardly realised when out tumbled nothing more interesting than a collection of thirteen leatherbound papyrus books, together with some loose sheets of papyrus. The find was so little valued that the loose papyri soon went up in smoke as firelighters.

However, one of the several tangled elements to the story is the fact that a few months earlier Muhammad 'Ali and his brothers had become embroiled in a series of revenge killings, following the murder of their father. Because of repeated police raids and periods of detention, some of the books were left with a local priest for safe-keeping. At the priest's house a local history teacher happened to see one of these. Suspecting it might have some cash value he took it to a doctor friend interested in the Coptic language, who in his turn contacted the Department of Antiquities. Although they swiftly purchased this book, it emerged that the remainder of the collection had meanwhile been scattered, changing hands often for trifling sums. It took several years of detective work and bargainings, during which one of the manuscripts was

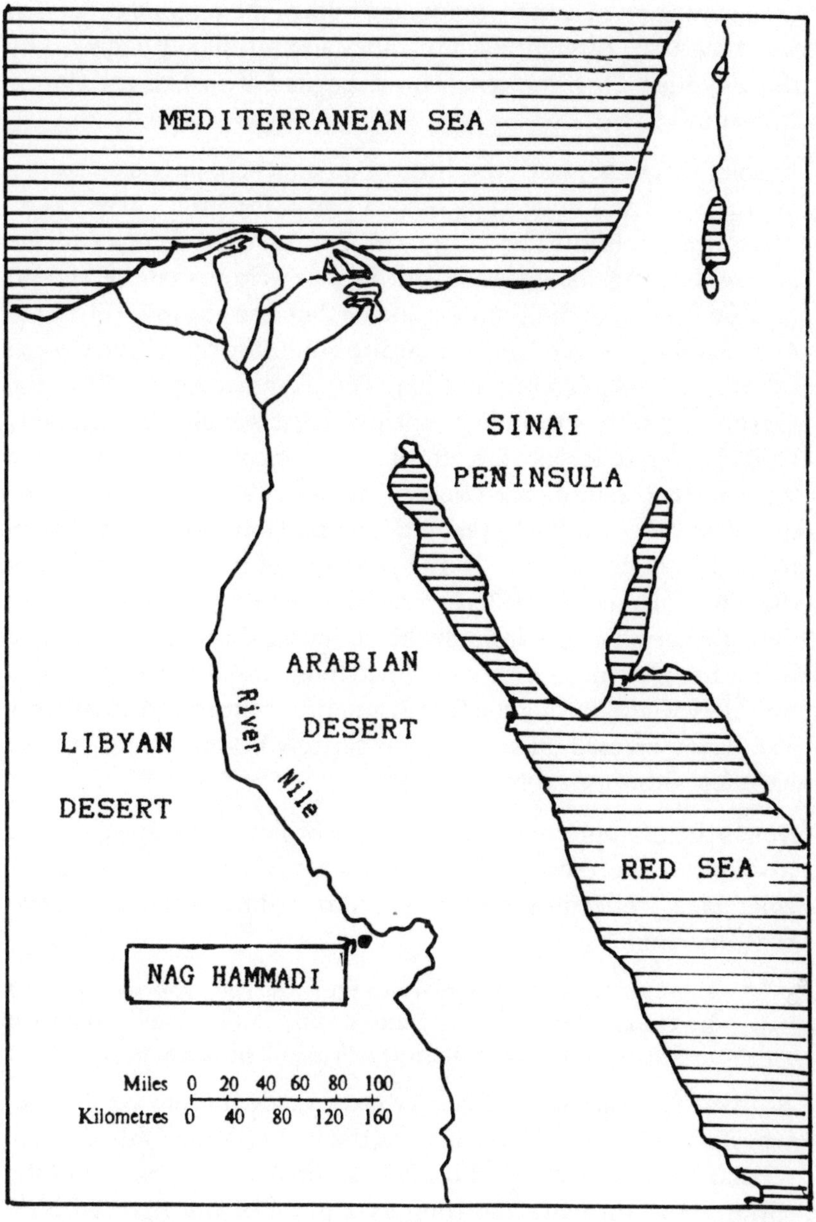

Figure 4. The site of discovery of the Nag Hammadi manuscript collection.

even smuggled to Zurich, before the bulk of the original collection was eventually brought back together and ultimately acquired by the Egyptian Government, who deposited it in Cairo's Coptic Museum.

Even at this stage, however, little of the first scholarly inspections of the collection suggested special cause for excitement. The books were found to be written in Coptic, the successor to the ancient Egyptian language. From datable written materials found re-used for the bindings they could be dated to around AD 350 to 400. Although several had promising-sounding titles – the Gospel of Philip, the Apocryphon of James, the Apocalypse of Paul, the Gospel of Truth and similar – their content was almost invariably typical of the apocryphal flights of fancy concocted by the Gnostic sects of Christianity's early years. Just above the site of the books' discovery there are 5,000 year old Egyptian tombs which had been robbed in antiquity, and at the time of the books' composition these would have made ideal spiritual retreats for solitude-seeking Gnostic hermits. Accordingly the books most probably belonged to one or more such Gnostic-inclined monks who buried the cache for safety when, during the fourth and fifth centuries, Christianity as a newly-created official religion actively began to root out the heresies within its ranks.

But as photographs of the manuscripts began to become available to scholars, interest slowly began to focus on one of five texts inside what has now become known as Codex 2 of the collection, a text commencing:

> These are the secret words which the living Jesus spoke, and which the twin, Judas Thomas, wrote down. And he said: 'Whoever discovers the meaning of these words will not taste death'. [2]

At first this reference to 'secret words' made it seem yet another Gnostic work, and indeed this was the first opinion of the French scholar Jean Doresse,[3] who made a cursory examination in the spring of 1949, while studying as a pupil of the Parisian New Testament scholar H.C. Puech. But in 1952, while happening to re-read Doresse's notes, Puech suddenly recognised that the

Coptic passage about the 'secret words' was one and the same as the fragmentary passage in Greek on one of the extra pages from the mysterious gospel which Grenfell and Hunt had unearthed at Oxyrhynchus at the beginning of the century.

Then in 1955, having become aware of Puech's interpretation, Gilles Quispel, Professor of the History of Religion at the University of Utrecht, specially travelled to Cairo to become the first major scholar to study the complete text. Only at this point did the Nag Hammadi's gospel's potential significance become fully realised.

For as Quispel quickly recognised,[4] unlike the mere fragments that had been found at Oxyrhynchus, here was the complete book, consisting of no less than 114 sayings of Jesus, several of these hitherto quite unknown. Also quite apparent was that this was certainly not the lost 'Gospel of the Hebrews'. Not only did it not contain such known elements of 'Hebrews' as the adulterous woman story, and Jesus's appearance to James, the very opening sentence specifically accredited it to Jesus's famous 'doubting' disciple Thomas. So the question now raised was whether this gospel was genuinely a collection of Jesus's sayings as made by the disciple Thomas himself, or whether it was just another apocryphal pretence at this.

Now Thomas as an historical individual has some considerable interest. His name is an Aramaic one which literally means 'Twin', so that when John's gospel refers to him as 'Thomas, known as the Twin' (Didymus) (John 11:16) this is simply a translation of the name into Greek. Although in fact only the John gospel gives Thomas any special attention, in Chapter 14 of this he is quoted as asking the question that prompts Jesus's famous statement, 'I am the Way, the Truth and the Life' (John 14:5). And in Chapter 20 it is Thomas who, after touching the wounds of the resurrected Jesus, becomes the first man in history unequivocally to acknowledge Jesus's divinity with the exclamation: 'My Lord and my God!' (John 20:28).

Intriguingly, while several of Jesus's disciples fade into obscurity in the aftermath of the Crucifixion, this does not seem to have

AUGUSTANA UNIVERSITY COLLEGE
LIBRARY

been the case with Thomas. According to the ever-helpful Bishop Eusebius of Caesarea's *History of the Church*, Thomas went off to evangelise in Parthia,[5] the empire that in the first century was Rome's immediate eastern neighbour. An even more intriguing, and not totally impossible, tradition also associates Thomas with the evangelisation of the southern part of India. When the Portuguese landed on India's Malabar coast in 1501 they were astonished to find a long-established and orthodox Christian community claiming its descent specifically from Thomas's evangelism.[6] And an apocryphal but not totally incredible *Acts of St Thomas*, certainly written before the middle of the third century AD, describes at considerable length Thomas's mission to an undeniably historical first-century King Gundaphor of India.[7]

Now it is important to be as cautious about such stories as about crediting any non-canonical gospel to Thomas's authorship. There has long been known among Christian apocrypha another 'Gospel of Thomas' consisting of a collection of stories of Jesus's boyhood whose fanciful and arguably Gnostic nature is quite evident even from a very casual extract:

> The little child Jesus when he was five years old was playing at the ford of a brook: and he gathered together the waters that flowed there into pools, and made them straightway clean, and commanded them by his word alone. And having made soft clay, he fashioned thereof twelve sparrows. And it was the sabbath when he did these things.[8]

Scholars have also long been aware that some form of gospel attributed to Thomas, whether the 'Jesus's boyhood' one, or the Nag Hammadi collection of sayings, was known to the early Church fathers, and forthrightly condemned by them. A 'Thomas' gospel is for instance one of those listed in the *Decretum Gelasianum*. According to Cyril, the fourth-century Bishop of Jerusalem, it was the work of the heretic Manichees:

> The Manichaeans also wrote a Gospel according to Thomas, which though coloured with the fragrance of a gospel name, corrupts the souls of the simpler.[9]

> Let no one read the Gospel according to Thomas, for it is not by one of the twelve apostles, but by one of the three wicked disciples of Manes.[10]

But there is good reason to believe that this Manichaean gospel cannot have been the same as the one represented in the Nag Hammadi and Oxyrhynchus texts. Instead the Manichees were most likely responsible for the version with the stories of Jesus's boyhood. This is not least for the simple reason that the Oxyrhynchus manuscript can confidently be dated no later than AD 200, fifteen years before the notorious Manes (circa AD 215 to 275), founder of the Manichaeans, had even been born, let alone begun to gather disciples.

However, the crucial question, independent of the historicity or otherwise of Thomas's evangelical missions and/or any other texts credited to him, is whether the historical disciple Thomas could actually have written the original gospel as preserved in the Oxyrhynchus and Nag Hammadi texts. And even if he did not, just as the tax-collector disciple Matthew most likely did not write the canonical gospel that bears his name, nonetheless does the 'Thomas' gospel contain unknown sayings genuinely once uttered by Jesus?

First, there can be no doubt that the 'Thomas' gospel certainly attributes to Jesus several credible-sounding sayings that are unknown from any other source.

Unlike the canonical gospels, for instance, but readily in line with what we have learned of the 'Gospel of the Hebrews', the 'Thomas' gospel gives some special attention to James, brother of Jesus. This is quite evident from Saying 11:

> The disciples said to Jesus, 'We know that you will depart from us. Who is to be our leader?'. Jesus said to them, 'Wherever you are you are to go to James the Righteous, for whose sake heaven and earth came into being'.

Although some have suggested that the use of the term 'the Righteous' suggests a dating of some time later than the first century, in fact the second-century Hegesippus, according to the extract preserved by Eusebius, specifically remarked of James that 'everyone from the Lord's time till our own has called [him] the Righteous.' The same term was also apparently used by James's direct contemporary, the non-Christian first-century Jewish historian Josephus.[11] And the phrase 'for whose sake heaven and earth came into being', while strange to anyone familiar only with the canonical gospels, is in fact rather characteristically Jewish. Passages in the Jewish Talmud similarly refer to creation having taken place for Moses, for Moses and Aaron, for Abraham, and for King David and the coming Messiah.

Furthermore, many of the 'Thomas' gospel's sayings have the authority, simplicity and directness that we have come to associate with utterances genuinely attributable to Jesus. Saying 17 is an interesting case in point:

> Jesus said:
> I shall give you
> what no eye has seen
> and what no ear has heard
> and what no hand has touched
> and what has never occurred to the human mind.

Although this partly harks back to Isaiah 64:3, it has that extra twist typical of Jesus. And Paul in his first letter to the Corinthians seemed specifically to have heard this saying as an utterance from Jesus when he wrote:

> ... as it is written
> What eye has never seen, nor ear heard,
> What has never entered the mind of man
> God has prepared for those who love him.
>
> (I Corinthians 2:9)

Similar circumstances apply to the 'Thomas' gospel's Saying 22:

> Jesus saw infants being suckled. He said to his disciples, 'These infants being suckled are like those who enter the Kingdom'.
>
> They said to him, 'Shall we then, as children, enter the Kingdom?'.

> Jesus said to them, 'When you make the two one and when you make the inside like the outside, and the outside like the inside, and the above like the below, and when you make the male and the female one and the same, so that the male not be male nor the female female ... then you will enter [the Kingdom]'.

While this passage likewise has no parallel in the canonical gospels, a hint that Jesus genuinely said something of this kind can again be gleaned from Paul, this time from his letter to the Galatians, written around AD 57, and therefore most likely before any of the canonical gospels had been written. In this he quite specifically remarked:

> All baptised in Christ ... there are no more distinctions between Jew and Greek, slave and free, *male and female*, but all of you are one ... [italics mine]
>
> (Galatians 3:28)

Even where the 'Thomas' gospel does in many instances give sayings that have parallels in the canonical gospels, there are few if any indications that its author has copied or in any way been influenced by these latter. Rather, where direct comparisons are possible, the 'Thomas' version often seems to provide a simpler, and therefore arguably more original form.

A typical case in point derives from comparison between the Luke and Matthew versions of the parable of the invited guests (Matthew 22:1-10 and Luke 14:16-24), and that of the 'Thomas' gospel. In the Matthew version this particular parable is unusually long, with the feast given by a king, who has arranged it for his son's wedding. When the invited guests do not come, and some even kill the servants sent out with the invitations, the furious king sends out troops to punish the wrongdoers, and more servants to invite all and sundry in their stead. Then when one of the newly invited guests arrives without the proper wedding attire, this guest in his turn is punished. Unusually among the canonical parables this one seems over-elaborate, and although Luke's version is notably simpler, without the element of kings and troops, even this has the somewhat jarring element of servants forcing individuals to come to the feast. Overall both canonical versions have an air of the story having gone wrong somewhere in the re-telling.

By contrast the 'Thomas' version, represented in Saying 64, has a greater simplicity that seems to bring us much closer to the original form in which Jesus might have given it:

> Jesus said, 'A man had received visitors. And when he had prepared the dinner, he sent his servant to invite the guests. He went to the first one and said to him, "My master invites you". He said, "I have claims against some merchants. They are coming to me this evening. I must go and give them my orders. I ask to be excused from the dinner". He went to another and said to him, "My master has invited you". He said to him, "I have just bought a house and am required for the day. I shall not have any spare time". ... He went to another and said to him, "My master invites you". He said to him, "I have just bought a farm and I am on my way to collect the rent. I shall not be able to come. I ask to be excused". The servant returned and said to his master, "Those whom you invited to the dinner have asked to be excused". The master said to his servant, "Go outside to the streets and bring back those whom you happen to meet, so that they may dine. Businessmen and merchants will not enter the places of my Father"'.

Here we seem to have a straight, very credibly Jesus-like parable with none of Matthew's window-dressing of a king and troops, nor Luke's element of force. And the same pertains to another parable, that of the wicked husbandmen of Mark 12:1–12; Matthew 21:33–46; and Luke 20:9–19. Again 'Thomas', in Saying 65, has the simplest, and therefore arguably the most authentic version:

> He [Jesus] said, 'There was a good man who owned a vineyard. He leased it to tenant farmers so that they might work it and he might collect the produce from them. He sent his servant so that the tenants might give him the produce of the vineyard. They seized his servant and beat him, all but killing him. The servant went back and told his master. The master said, "Perhaps [they] did not recognise [him]". He sent another servant. The tenants beat this one as well. Then the owner sent his son and said, "Perhaps they will show respect to my son". Because the tenants knew that it was

> he who was the heir to the vineyard, they seized him and killed him. Let him who has ears hear'.

Even so, it is important not to be beguiled by such features into too readily accepting that the 'Thomas' gospel somehow contains *in toto* just what we have been looking for, that is, an authentic collection of words of Jesus, including many unrecorded in the canonical gospels. For also quite evident from the Nag Hammadi text is that a considerable portion of the unfamiliar material conveys ideas that do not ring quite right, and strongly suggests the same Gnosticism as the rest of the hoard found with this particular manuscript.

Thus the very opening paragraph, for instance, describes the gospel as 'secret', which raises again the still unresolved question of whether Jesus did or did not give his disciples special teaching that was not for public dissemination. As noted earlier, in Mark's gospel Jesus quite specifically tells 'the Twelve, together with the others who formed his company':

> The secret of the kingdom of God is given to you, but to those who are outside everything comes in parables.
>
> (Mark 4:11)

Yet in apparent contradiction to this John's gospel represents Jesus insisting at the time of his arrest:

> I have spoken openly for all the world to hear; I have always taught in the synagogue and in the Temple where all the Jews meet together; I have said nothing in secret.
>
> (John 18:20)

The only apparent way to resolve this impasse is to focus attention on the question – one which theologians have long argued over quite aside from any non-canonical texts – of what exactly might have been (or still be) this 'secret of the kingdom of God' as so cryptically alluded to by Mark. Luke 17:21 says, 'The kingdom of God is within you' (or more literally 'among you') and the Nag Hammadi 'Thomas' seems encouragingly to expand this a little in its Saying 3:

> If those who lead you say to you, 'See the Kingdom is in the sky,' then the birds of the sky will precede you. If they say to you, 'It is in the sea,' then the fish will precede you. Rather the kingdom is inside of you and it is outside of you.

But here a disturbing feature arises from comparison of this, the Coptic text, with its albeit fragmentary Greek equivalent from the scrap Grenfell and Hunt found at Oxyrhynchus:

> Jesus said [...
> who draw us ...
> the kingdom in heaven ...
> the birds of the heaven
> what under the earth ...
> the fishes of the sea ...
> you, and the kingdom ...
> is within you ...
> know, will find it ... the

Despite the Oxyrhynchus text's incompleteness, it seems evident that, unlike the later one from Nag Hammadi, it did not include the element of the kingdom being 'outside of you', an idea much more characteristically Gnostic. And this raises the question of what other Gnostic elements might have been added or changed by whoever was responsible for rendering what may still have been genuinely early gospel into Coptic.

Inevitably, because we lack a correspondingly complete version of the original Greek text to compare with the Coptic one, it is impossible to determine exactly what changes may have been introduced. But nonetheless there are other definite signs of these. In the case of Saying 36, for instance:

> Jesus said: 'Do not be concerned from morning until evening and from evening till morning about what you will wear'.

the Greek version has the additional lines, all paralleled in Matthew and Luke:

> You are much better than the lilies, which neither card, nor spin...
>
> Having one garment, who do you ...?

> Who would add to your stature?
>
> He himself will give you your garment.

It is accordingly apparent that for some undetermined reason, but arguably deliberately, the Coptic editor/translator omitted this from the Nag Hammadi version.

Similarly where at the end of Saying 5 the Coptic text reads: '... there is nothing hidden which will not become manifest', the Greek version has in addition: 'there is nothing buried which will not ...'.

Although yet again a word is missing here, it can almost certainly be reconstructed from an inscription found on a fifth/sixth-century grave wrapping from Oxyrhynchus: 'Jesus says, "There is nothing buried which will not be raised"'. [12]

As remarked by New Testament scholar Robert M. Grant of the University of Chicago:

> If this was the original reading of Thomas, then we have clear evidence of Gnostic removal of a reference to the resurrection. It is Gnostic because Gnostics insisted on the survival of the spirit, not the resurrection of the body.[13]

Accordingly, the bad news for us is that while the Nag Hammadi Coptic text might appear to have given us a complete copy of the 'Thomas' gospel, indisputably the text appears to have undergone some serious tampering at Gnostic hands. At this point therefore, in order to determine the extent of this, and thus better to identify those sayings not interfered with in this way, there may be some value in temporarily diverting our attention to the extent of the Gnostic character of some of the other works, besides the 'Thomas' gospel, that appear in the Nag Hammadi collection.

Chapter 6

More Words from Nag Hammadi

In all, the twelve papyrus books and remains of a thirteenth that survive from whatever may have been the full contents of Muhammad 'Ali's jar comprise no less than 52 separate texts, including six repeats. Although some of the texts are fragmentary, altogether they furnish some forty ancient books of a religious nature that were previously either unknown, or had been thought lost for ever. But as already indicated, the bulk of these offer little of any interest except to the most specialist enthusiast for Gnosticism.

First, for instance, there is a substantial proportion of the material that cannot be considered even marginally Christian. One such is the 'Three Steles of Seth', comprising non-Christian hymns seemingly used as aids to meditation. Another, 'On the Eighth and the Ninth' is a dialogue between the pagan diety Hermes Trismegistus and a son or pupil concerning how to ascend to the heavenly spheres. 'Asklepios' is another Hermetic dialogue, this time one between Hermes and the Greek healing deity Asklepios. 'The Paraphrase of Shem' is all about the conflict between the primeval forces of Light, Darkness and Spirit. One book even consists of a fragmentary and appallingly translated extract from Plato's *Republic*.

Only slightly less pagan are works such as the 'Apocalypse of Adam' and the 'Apocryphon of John'. The former at least features the familiar figures of Adam and Eve. The latter is a Gnostic version of a commentary on the Book of Genesis, portraying the God of Genesis as having blinded man from knowledge of his true identity, and the Saviour as the one whose main role was to re-awaken that knowledge.

Beginning to be at least slightly Christian, though still heretical to the orthodox both then and now, are those works in the collection that may best be described as Docetic. As noted earlier, the essential feature of these is the idea that the Jesus who walked the earth during the early years of the first century AD only had the semblance of a flesh and blood human being. According to this mode of thinking, in reality Jesus was an entirely spiritual being who therefore did not actually have to suffer any of the pain of the Crucifixion; all this was only an appearance, a sham. A typical example of this occurs in the Nag Hammadi book entitled 'The Second Treatise to the Great Seth' in which Jesus is represented as telling a group of Gnostic disciples:

> For my death, which they think happened, happened to them in their error and blindness, since they nailed their man unto their death. It was another upon whom they placed the crown of thorns. But I was rejoicing in the height over all the wealth of the archons and the offspring of their error, of their empty glory. And I was laughing at their ignorance.[1]

Given such a plethora of arcane, other-worldly material so alien to normal Christian thinking, even the more promisingly Christian-sounding titles in the Nag Hammadi collection offer little glimmer of more down-to-earth content. One of the works that is duplicated in the Nag Hammadi collection, and must therefore clearly have been popular, is a 'Gospel of the Egyptians'. But this cannot be one and the same as the work of this title already noted as having been referred to by some of the early Church fathers. The Nag Hammadi version contains none of the passages which we already know of from the latter (see pages 40,41). Instead it is yet more esoteric and dominated by symbolism than most other works in the collection.

Only just a trifle more Christian is a fragmentary work, housed within the same codex as the 'Gospel of the Egyptians', seemingly promisingly entitled 'The Dialogue of the Saviour'.[2] Although Jesus is referred to in this either as 'the Saviour' or 'the Lord', rather than directly by name, nonetheless it consists of a lot of otherwise unfamiliar utterances attributed to him, purportedly as given to three disciples, Judas, Mary and Matthew.

But disappointingly, there is nothing in these utterances suggestive of anything we can easily believe he actually said considering what we learned of him in Chapter 2. Instead they consist of answers to questions on esoteric matters purportedly put to him after his resurrection, and very unconvincing ones at that:

> [Matthew] said, 'Lord, I want [to see] that place of life [...] where there is no wickedness, [but rather] there is pure [light]'. The Lord [said], 'Brother [Matthew], you will not be able to see it [as long as you are] carrying flesh around'.
>
> ('Dialogue' 27, 28)

Even in this short passage we see two characteristically Gnostic philosophic themes, that of the light, and that of the earthly body being a form of prison for the true spiritual body which lies beneath. Here the qualification does need to be made that neither theme is entirely alien to sayings of Jesus and to mainstream Christianity. One of the most famous passages in the entire New Testament is the opening of John's gospel:

> All that came to be had life in him,
> and that life was the light of men,
> a light that shines in the dark,
> a light that darkness could not overpower.
>
> (John 1:4–5)

Even Jesus himself uses such 'light' imagery in some passages of the synoptic gospels, such as Matthew 6:22–3:

> If your eye is sound, your whole body will be filled with light. But if your eye is diseased, your whole body will be all darkness. If then the light inside you is darkness, what darkness that will be!

Similarly, in regard to the concept of the prison of the flesh, among Paul's most famous words are those from his first letter to the Corinthians:

> Flesh and blood cannot inherit the kingdom of God.
>
> (I Corinthians 15:50).

But there is a fundamental difference to these themes as they recur virtually *ad nauseam* in Gnostic literature such as the 'Dialogue'.

In the Gnostic works the light is locked in a primeval, cosmological battle with the darkness that is rooted in pagan philosophical concepts. One of many examples of this is the way the theme appears in the 'Apocryphon of John', which has already been noted as bearing very little relation to anything recognisably Christian.

> I am the light which exists in the light. I am the remembrance of the Providence.
>
> ('Apocryphon of John')

Another heavily Gnostic and unconvincing saying attributed to Jesus in the 'Dialogue' extols the value of knowledge:

> If [one] does not [understand how] fire came into existence, he will burn in it, because he does not know the root of it. If one does not first understand water, he knows nothing. For what use is there for him to be baptised in it? If one does not understand how blowing wind came into existence, he will blow away with it. If one does not understand how body, which he bears, came into existence, he will [perish] with it ....
>
> ('Dialogue' 35)

In another example in the 'Dialogue', after a question by Matthew about life after death, Jesus is reported to reply:

> [You have] asked me about a saying [...] which eye has not seen, [nor] have I heard it except from you. But I say to you that when what invigorates a man is removed, he will be called 'dead'. And when what is alive leaves what is dead, what is alive will be called upon.
>
> ('Dialogue' 57)

This is typical Gnostic 'philosophy', lacking anything of the distinctive touches of imagery with which the real Jesus illustrated and explained virtually everything he said. And two verses later we find this pastiche 'Jesus' supposedly giving voice to one of the already noted anti-feminist ideas with which Gnosticism was tinged:

> Whatever is born of truth does not die. Whatever is born of woman dies.
>
> ('Dialogue' 59)

This theme also recurs again in a saying attributed to Jesus towards the end of the 'Dialogue':

> The Lord said, 'Pray in the place where there is no woman'.
>
> ('Dialogue' 91)

While, therefore, a work specifically entitled the 'Dialogue of the Saviour' might reasonably be expected to offer some convincing sayings of Jesus independent of the gospels, in reality this is not the case. Nor does the Nag Hammadi so-called 'Gospel of Philip'[3], which immediately follows that of 'Thomas' in the collection's second codex, offer much more encouragement. Even though, like so much else among the Nag Hammadi and other Gnostic material, this too has nothing of the narrative framework of the canonical gospels, it does at least include some familiar sayings of Jesus recognisable from the latter.

Thus we can find a reference to the Lord's Prayer, to the parable of the Good Samaritan, to Jesus's remarks on praying in secret (Matthew 6:6), and to the John's gospel sayings 'If you do not eat the flesh of the Son of Man ...' (John 6:53) and 'Everyone who commits sin is a slave', (John 8:34). These are among several indications that this 'gospel' was composed some while after the creation and dissemination of the famous four.

But since this 'Philip' gospel also has several sayings that are not known from the canonicals, we might therefore be lulled into thinking that these could be genuine new material. Regrettably, however, once these latter are properly scrutinised, it soon becomes obvious that they raise virtually no such hopes:

> The Lord said to the disciples, '[...] from every house. Bring into the house of my father. But do not take [anything] in the house of the father nor carry it off'.
>
> (Philip 55:37 to 56:3)

> He said on that day in the thanksgiving, 'You who have joined the perfect light with the holy spirit, unite the angels with us also, as being the images'.
>
> (Philip 58:10–14)

> ... a disciple asked the Lord one day for something of this world. He said to him, 'Ask your mother, and she will give you of the things which are another's'.
>
> (Philip 59:25–27)

> The Lord went into the dye works of Levi. He took seventy-two different colours and threw them into the vat. He took them out all white. And he said, 'Even so has the son of man come as a dyer'.
>
> (Philip 63:29,30)

> [The Lord loved] Mary Magdalen ... more than [all] the disciples [and used to] kiss her [often] on her [...] The rest of [the disciples...] They said to him, 'Why do you love her more than all of us?' The Saviour answered and said to them, 'Why do I not love you like her? When a blind man and one who sees are both together in darkness, they are no different from one another. When the light comes, then he who sees will see the light, and he who is blind will remain in darkness'.
>
> (Philip 64:2–9)

> The Lord said, 'Blessed is he who is before he came into being. For he who is, has been and shall be'.
>
> (Philip 64:10–12)

> [...] he said, 'I came to make [the things below] like the things [above, and the things] outside like those [inside. I came to unite] them in the place'.
>
> (Philip 67:30–35)

> The Lord said it well: 'Some have entered the kingdom of heaven laughing, and they have come out [...] because [...] a Christian, [...]'.
>
> (Philip 74:25–27)

Where these sayings are not either too fragmentary to be intelligible, or locked in the obscurity so typical of Gnosticism, they still have overtly Gnostic themes, as in the second saying's reference to the 'light' (Philip 58:10-14). And while the story of Jesus's favouritism towards Mary Magdalen, followed by the saying concerning the blind man, might seem to offer just a whisker of a resemblance to what might be expected from Jesus, a little further reflection reveals that it is merely another play on the Gnostics' favourite light theme. It totally lacks that original and distinctive twist which in the canonicals is so frequently a hallmark of Jesus's true authorship.

Here also we come face to face with the fact that not least of the problems associated with all the Nag Hammadi books (with the notable exception of 'Thomas'), is the consistently esoteric, rambling and unfocused way in which they have been written. This is almost certainly a hallmark of the dreamy unworldliness which Gnostics affected, and in this regard it should not necessarily be too stridently condemned. After all, there is really little to distinguish it from, for instance, that spirit-inspired imagination that was to typify the art and writings of the English poet William Blake a millennium and a half later.

But what is important is that we should not even begin to be seduced into accepting any historical validity for the vast majority of Gnostic literature's purported sayings of Jesus, any more than mainstream Christians of the early centuries were prepared to accept the Gnostics themselves. Even from as early as the writing of the New Testament's Second Letter of St Paul to Timothy, probably written by a second-century Christian rather than by Paul himself, there is special criticism of the activities of two seeming Gnostics of that time:

> Have nothing to do with pointless philosophical discussions - they only lead further and further away from true religion. Talk of this kind corrodes like gangrene, as in the case of Hymenaeus and Philetus, the men who have gone right away from truth and claim that the resurrection has already taken place. Some people's faith cannot stand up to them.
>
> (2 Timothy 2:16–18)

Similarly, the fourth-century Cypriot Bishop Epiphanius, who seems to have come across Gnosticism in Egypt during very much the era when the Nag Hammadi books were produced, remarked:

> For I happened on this sect myself, and was actually taught these things in person, out of the mouths of practising Gnostics. Not only did women under this delusion offer me this line of talk, and divulge this sort of thing to me. With impudent boldness,

> moreover, they tried to seduce me themselves ... But the merciful God rescued me from their wickednesses, and thus - after reading them and their books, understanding their true intent and not being carried away with them, and after escaping without taking the bait - I lost no time reporting them to the bishops there, and finding out which ones were hidden in the Church. Thus they were expelled from the city, about eighty persons, and the city was cleared of their tare-like, thorny growth.[4]

Yet what should not be overlooked in all this is that it is most unlikely that Christian Gnosticism sprang out of nothing. Just as we have seen that the Gnostics' favourite themes are not totally alien to the gospels, so there is likely to have been at least something in Jesus's original teaching which provided the root-stock to which Gnosticism's weeds latched themselves.

Here the 'Thomas' gospel, with a content so much more ordered and credible than anything else in the Nag Hammadi collection, yet a disturbing claim to represent 'secret' teaching of Jesus, seems to confront us with the very touchstone of this mystery. As remarked in the previous chapter, simple comparison of the Nag Hammadi Coptic text with the Greek of the Oxyrhynchus fragments leaves no doubt that the Coptic version has suffered some significant adulteration at Gnostic hands, as for example the already noted removal of reference to the resurrection of the body.

But there are also certain passages, even in the Coptic version of 'Thomas', that are unknown from the canonicals, have a primitive 'feel' of the original Jesus, yet also seem to lend themselves as ideas subsequently over-cultivated in Gnosticism proper. Much earlier in this book we noted the originality Jesus brought to the parable, in which context of particular interest is a hitherto quite unknown and initially somewhat obscure parable that appears in 'Thomas' as Sayings 97 and 98:

> Jesus said, 'The kingdom of the [father] is like a certain woman who was carrying a [jar] full of meal. While she was walking [on the] road, still some distance from home, the handle of the jar broke and the meal emptied out behind her [on] the road. She did not realise it; she had noticed no accident. When she reached her

> house, she set the jar down and found it empty'.
>
> Jesus said, 'The kingdom of the father is like a certain man who wanted to kill a powerful man. In his own house he drew his sword and stuck it into the wall in order to find out whether his hand could carry through. Then he slew the powerful man'.

First, an unusual feature is that these two apparently independent analogous-style sayings actually belong together as one parable that is only properly intelligible by their juxtaposition. The key lies in the house, the setting which each saying shares, and which represents the earthly existence. The woman, with every appearance of worthiness, has gathered all the material she needs (the meal) to take to this house, and has conscientiously carried this along, only to find at the end of her journey that it is all as nothing. Her error, just as Martha in Luke 10:38–42, has been to see the house as the goal of her existence.

By contrast the man, although he seems altogether less worthy with his intentions of destruction, is already inside the house, and is all-importantly looking outward from it. He sees the 'powerful man' as the barrier between him and his true goal of the kingdom of heaven, and he correctly uses the house merely as a vessel upon which to test his strength before overcoming the barrier effectively. Unlike the woman he does not cling to life. He sees it as a testing-ground for the world beyond, rather than as an end in itself.

Not only does this have just the sort of double-thinking avoidance of the obvious features that we have learned is so typical of Jesus, an important cross-check of Jesus's authorship is to be found in Luke 14:31:

> 'What king marching to war against another king would not first sit down and consider whether with ten thousand men he could stand up to the other who advanced against him with twenty thousand?'.

This is not only a direct parallel to 'Thomas''s 'powerful man' analogy; the context for this 'testing' imagery is also exactly the same: the theme of renunciation of worldly possessions and worldly ties. Just as the parable in the 'Thomas' is almost immediately preceded by the saying:

> If you have money, do not lend it at interest, but give to one from whom you will not get it back.
>
> ('Thomas', Saying 95)

almost immediately before in Luke, Jesus exhorts concerning invited guests:

> When you have a party, invite the poor, the crippled, the lame, the blind, that they cannot pay you back...
>
> (Luke 14:14)

Both the Luke and 'Thomas' gospels include in almost equally close proximity Jesus's harsh words on the necessity of renouncing all that one holds dear:

> If any man comes to me without hating his father, mother, wife, children, brothers, sisters, yes and his own life too, he cannot be my disciple.
>
> (Luke 14:25-27)

> Whoever does not hate his [father] and his mother as I do cannot become a [disciple] to me.
>
> ('Thomas', Saying 101)

And leaving absolutely no doubt that the parable's theme is the renunciation of possessions, Luke includes at the very end of Jesus's saying concerning the king weighing up the strength of his army the further words:

> So in the same way none of you can be my disciple unless he gives up all his possessions.

An important point here is that since Luke does not have 'Thomas''s counterpoised element of the woman with the emptying jar, in Luke the saying has not only lost its apparent original setting as part of a parable, it *has* to be explained. Arguably this was a loss which occurred in transmission, just as we had noted earlier of the distortions to the canonical tenant-farmers and the king's wedding-feast parables. This in turn means that at least in the case of this element of the 'Thomas' gospel we hear something of Jesus's words rather better than in any surviving gospel. One of his otherwise lost parables has actually been restored to us ...

The 'Thomas' gospel is then of priceless importance in having as at least part of its content some rich source material antedating the canonical gospels, source material seemingly on a par with the 'Matthew' sayings and the hypothetical 'Q' referred to in Chapter 1. Furthermore, in whatever can be construed of the original form of this, it would seem to be a parallel to John's gospel in concentrating its sights on Jesus's more special teachings concerned with the nature of eternal life, rather than the earthly existence. Thus just as John quotes of Jesus:

> It is the spirit that gives life;
> the flesh has nothing to offer.
> The words I have spoken to you are spirit,
> and they are life.
>
> (John 6:63)

so Jesus's very first saying in the *Thomas* gospel is:

> Whoever finds the interpretation of these sayings will not experience death.

Having said this, any idea that the 'Thomas' gospel might be considered on any sort of par with that of John should be very quickly dismissed. At best it gives us merely a few raw, shorthand notebook jottings that were mislaid or otherwise omitted from the altogether more polished works of the canonicals.

But even these can offer a new insight hitherto lacking, in which context of special interest are those elements of the 'Thomas' gospel known from the second-century Oxyrhynchus text, and therefore arguably the least likely to have suffered Gnostic tampering. Earlier we remarked that the Oxyrhynchus text included the passage 'You are much better than the lilies ...', and that this was for some reason omitted from the Nag Hammadi version. In fact this particular passage derived from eight fragments of the same gospel which came to light in 1903 at the Oxyrhynchus site in 1903, six years after Hunt's 'karphos' find. Immediately following the lilies passage is legible in the Greek:

> They say to him, his disciples, 'When will you be visible to us and when shall we see you?'. He says, 'When you are stripped and are not ashamed ...'.

And here the Coptic version fills in for us what has become lost by the erosion of centuries in the case of the Greek:

> His disciples said, 'When will you become revealed to us and when shall we see you?'. Jesus said, 'When you disrobe without being ashamed and take up your garments and place them under your feet like little children and tread on them, then [will you see] the Son of the Living One ...'.
>
> ('Thomas', Saying 37)

Saying 21 echoes the same idea:

> Mary said to Jesus, 'Whom are your disciples like?'. He said, 'They are like children who have settled in a field which is not theirs. When the owners of the field come, they will say, "Let us have back our field". They [will] undress in their presence in order to let them have back their field and to give it back to them'.

Now curiously here we meet again the same seemingly Gnostic idea of unashamed nakedness first encountered in the extract from the (non-Nag Hammadi) 'Gospel of the Egyptians' quoted in Chapter 3.

> Salome asked when what she was inquiring about would be known.
>
> The Lord said, 'When you trample on the garment of shame, and when the two become one, and the male with the female neither male or female'.

Since this idea was clearly in the Greek version as well as the later Coptic version of the 'Thomas' gospel, the question arises as to whether it should be considered unacceptably Gnostic, in the sense of having been falsely attributed to Jesus, or whether we may have in the 'Thomas' gospel's Sayings 21 and 37 further genuine words of Jesus, possibly downplayed or neglected by the mainstream Church and the authors of the canonical gospels.

Here some further curiosities need to be noted. Besides Jesus's advocacy of lack of attention to clothing in his Sermon on the

Mount (Matthew 6:26–30 – the very passage which can be seen to have preceded 'Thomas' Saying 37 in the Oxyrhynchus text), in Mark's gospel the theme of innocent childlikeness is one that Jesus again quite specifically links to eligibility for the kingdom of God. Reproving his disciples for not allowing little children to come to him, Jesus tells them:

> Do not stop them; for it is to such as these that the kingdom of God belongs. I tell you solemnly, anyone who does not welcome the kingdom of God like a little child will never enter it.
>
> (Mark 10:14–15)

Undeniably in all versions Jesus's central theme was that his kingdom, one and the same as God's kingdom, where he would reveal himself, was already at hand. All that was needed was for the disciple figuratively, but nonetheless in a very real way, to strip himself of all worldly ties and trappings. But was this step (in actuality an enormous one) really intended only figuratively? It is to be recalled that in its very opening line 'Thomas''s gospel describes itself as 'the *secret* sayings which the living Jesus spoke.' So is it possible that, albeit as a symbolic preliminary to admission to his kingdom, Jesus expected an actual childlike stripping off of all clothing? Although from the 'Thomas' gospel alone this would be quite impossible to answer, a comparatively recent discovery of yet another source of lost words of Jesus has offered a quite extraordinary new key.

Chapter 7

Words from a Hitherto Unknown 'Secret Gospel'?

In 1941 Dr Morton Smith,[1] today Professor of Ancient History at New York's Columbia University, was stranded in Palestine, unable to return to the United States because of the Second World War. During this enforced period of absence he happened to be invited to stay for a few weeks at the Eastern Orthodox Church's great desert monastery of Mar Saba, a sister to the more famous St Catherine's of Mount Sinai. Here Smith found himself enchanted both by the monastery and the timelessness of the Orthodox monastic way of life, and was accordingly more than pleased when in 1958 he was invited to return, this time to study and catalogue the monastery's collection of manuscripts.

By contrast to the great St Catherine's, Mar Saba had in fact lost much of its former manuscript collection due to a great fire in the eighteenth century, and even many of its remaining manuscripts and books had been transferred to Jerusalem during the nineteenth. Even so Smith found some interesting items in a library in the monastery's old tower, and methodically began to sift through these during the summer of 1958.

As Smith found, because of shortage of paper in times past, the monks had sometimes copied passages into the end-papers of printed books or onto any other pages that had been left blank. Sometimes they had used old manuscripts as binding materials, one such that he happened to notice being a fifteenth-century copy of the works of Sophocles. Then one afternoon quite late in his stay Smith found himself staring at a Greek text that had been copied into the back of an otherwise unexceptional seventeenth-century printed edition of the letters of St Ignatius of Antioch. Although the writing was a tiny scrawl, he managed to decipher enough to recognise that it purported to be a letter 'of the most holy Clement', author of *The Stromateis*, seeming to praise a certain Theodore for having 'shut up' the Gnostic group known as the Carpocratians.

Smith knew this was likely to be an interesting find. Clement, author of *The Stromateis*, was none other than Clement of Alexandria, the well-known second-century Church father, whom we have already mentioned in respect of his preservation of an excerpt from the lost 'Gospel of the Egyptians'. Since Smith was fairly sure that none of Clement's letters were otherwise known to be preserved, the finding of a copy even as late as this one - the book itself was only seventeenth-century, so the writing inside had to be yet more recent - promised to be quite a coup. Accordingly Smith carefully photographed the text, then, when he had had the photographs developed, settled down to make a full translation from the Greek. At this stage nothing could have prepared him for the surprise the contents were about to reveal.

The first part was simply a preamble[2] in which Clement congratulated the unknown Theodore on how he had tackled 'the unspeakable teachings of the Carpocratians'. The Carpocratians, followers of a teacher called Carpocrates, are known to have been a Gnostic sect notorious for their sexual licentiousness. But then Clement went on:

> Now of the [things] they keep saying about the divinely inspired Gospel according to Mark, some are altogether falsifications, and others, even if they do contain some true [elements], nevertheless are not reported truly. For the true [things], being mixed with inventions, so that, as the saying [goes], even the salt loses its savour.
>
> [As for] Mark, then, during Peter's stay in Rome he wrote [an account of] the Lord's doings, not, however, declaring all [of them], nor yet hinting at the secret [ones], but selecting those he thought most useful for increasing the faith of those who were being instructed. But when Peter died as a martyr, Mark came over to Alexandria, bringing his own notes and those of Peter, from which he transferred to his former book the things suitable to whatever makes for progress towards knowledge [gnosis]. [Thus]

he composed a more spiritual gospel for the use of those who were being perfected ... and dying he left his composition to the church in Alexandria, where it even yet is most carefully guarded ...

But ... Carpocrates ... so enslaved a certain presbyter of the church in Alexandria that he got from him a copy of the secret Gospel, which he both interpreted according to his blasphemous and carnal doctrine and, moreoever, polluted, mixing with the spotless and holy words utterly shameless lies. From this mixture is drawn off the teaching of the Carpocratians.

To them, therefore ... one must never give way, nor ... should one concede that the secret Gospel is by Mark ... [But] to you ... I shall not hesitate to answer the [questions] you have asked, refuting the falsification by the very words of the Gospel. For example, after 'And they were in the road going up to Jerusalem,' and what follows, until 'After three days he shall arise,' [the secret Gospel] brings the following [material] word for word:

> And they came to Bethany, and a certain woman, whose brother had died, was there. And coming, she prostrated herself before Jesus and said to him, 'Son of David, have mercy on me'. But the disciples rebuked her. And Jesus, being angered, went off with her into the garden where the tomb was, and straightway a great cry was heard from the tomb. And going near, Jesus rolled away the stone from the door of the tomb. And straightway, going in where the youth was, he stretched forth his hand and raised him, seizing his hand. But the youth, looking upon him, loved him and began to beseech him that he might be with him. And going out of the tomb they came into the house of the youth, for he was rich. And after six days Jesus told him what to do and in the evening the youth came to him, wearing a linen cloth over [his] naked [body]. And he remained with him that night, for Jesus taught him the mystery of the kingdom of God. And thence, arising, he returned to the other side of the Jordan.

Clement went on:

After these [words] follows the text, 'And James and John come to him,' and all that section. But 'naked [man] with [naked] man' and the other things about which you wrote are not found. And after the [words] 'And he comes into Jericho' [the secret Gospel]

> adds only, 'And the sister of the youth whom Jesus loved, and his mother and Salome were there, and Jesus did not receive them'. But the many other [things about] which you wrote both seem to be and are falsifications. Now the true explanation and that which accords with the true philosophy ... [The text breaks here in the middle of a page.]

Now an immediate and riveting feature is that although it was clearly a long way removed from the Gnosticism of groups such as the Carpocratians, we seem from Clement's letter to have corroboration that there really was a 'secret', 'more spiritual' version of Jesus's teaching 'for the use of those who were being perfected', just as we have suspected from Thomas. It also seems apparent that associated with this teaching was some form of rite involving nudity.

Inevitably, before such ideas can even begin to be considered further, there are some key questions that need to be tackled. First, we need to know just what grounds there are for believing this eighteenth-century text to be a true copy of a letter genuinely once written by Clement of Alexandria in the second century. Second, even if we can be sure Clement of Alexandria did write it, we need to establish whether the extracts from what is quoted as the apparent 'secret' version of Mark could genuinely have been written by the evangelist of that name. In fact Smith has devoted a great deal of attention to both these questions.

For instance, with regard to the letter's authorship, Smith studied the vocabulary of Clement's three surviving works, the *Protepticus*, *Paedogogus*, and *Stromateis*, all of which have been preserved in manuscripts of the tenth and eleventh centuries. He concluded emphatically: 'The vocabulary of the letter is Clement's; almost all the words are words he uses and many of them are favourites of his, or are used in odd ways in which he also used them.' And he has found support for this view from several leading scholars, including the eminent Cambridge University professors Henry Chadwick and G.W.H. Lampe.

The indications are similarly positive with regard to the 'secret' gospel passages' authorship by Mark. Although not a great deal is known about the original canonical Mark, Acts 12:12 mentions a 'Mary, mother of John Mark' to whose apparently well-to-do house in Jerusalem (one that certainly employed servants) Peter went after escaping from prison. This same Mark seems to have accompanied Paul and Barnabas at the start of their first missionary journey, only to abandon them, apparently refusing 'to share in their work' when they reached the small town of Perga in the Roman province of Pamphylia, just inland from the southern coast of Turkey (Acts 13:13 ; 15:38). As earlier noted, Mark is then described by the early historian Papias as acting as secretary or interpreter for Peter during the latter's time in Rome.[3]

With regard to Clement's letter's statement that Mark ended his days in the Egyptian port of Alexandria, there is no known historical difficulty. We are freely told by our old friend the Church historian Bishop Eusebius of Caesarea:

> Mark is said to have been the first man to set out for Egypt and preach there the gospel which he had himself written down, and the first to establish churches in Alexandria itself.[4]

So was the evangelist Mark one and the same as whoever wrote the extract attributed to him in Morton Smith's 'secret gospel'? Here the passage quoted by Clement not only has the same overall simplicity of narrative quality as that of the canonical Mark, it also features such convincing touches as the mention of Jesus 'being angered'. However slight this might seem, it is a fact that neither Matthew, nor Luke nor John ever refers to Jesus being angry, due seemingly to a reluctance on their part (along with almost all later writers) to portray Jesus in anything less than a perfect light. But the canonical Mark does not shirk from mentioning Jesus's more human characteristics. And he quite specifically described Jesus as being angry at those critical of him for curing a man with a withered hand on the Sabbath:

> Grieved to find them so obstinate, he looked angrily round at them, and said to the man, 'Stretch out your hand'.
>
> (Mark 3:5)

Furthermore, that there genuinely was a 'secret' version of Mark's gospel would in fact explain several of the long-standing mysteries of its canonical version. One of the more minor ones is the peculiar statement of Chapter 10, verse 46: 'They reached Jericho, and as he left Jericho ...', which has always puzzled scholars regarding whatever might have happened in Jericho. 'Secret' Mark makes it clear that there was a sentence here concerning the visit of three women to tell him of the death of the young man whom, later in 'Secret' Mark, Jesus would raise from the dead. Without this latter story in the canonical version, the preliminary episode similarly had to be omitted, but was done sufficiently clumsily to leave signs of the removal.

But canonical Mark's most particular feature indicative that there really might have been a secret version is its quite unmistakable repeated emphasis on secrecy. One typical instance is the consistency with which demoniacs and others healed of diseases are instructed not to tell anyone what has happened to them, as in Mark 1:24; 1:44; 5:7; 5:43, and elsewhere. Another is the gospel's explicit statement by Jesus that the 'secret of the kingdom of God' is given directly to his disciples, but only via parables to 'those who are outside' (Mark 4:11).

Similarly pertinent is the fact that alone of the four gospels in its original form Mark did not include an account of Christianity's most central mystery and *raison d'être* – Jesus's Resurrection – arguably because the Resurrection was regarded as one of the higher mysteries. This would go some way to explaining the already noted and still puzzling fact that the earliest surviving texts of the canonical form of Mark, as preserved in the Codex Sinaiticus and others, all end abruptly at Chapter 16 verse 8, i.e. they include the women visiting Jesus's tomb being told of Jesus's Resurrection, but nothing of anyone seeing evidence of this with their own eyes. Although one possible explanation of this is simply that the end portion of Mark's original manuscript became lost at a very early stage, another, increasingly favoured, is that the truncation was quite deliberate, so that the officiating preacher could teach the higher mysteries of the faith more directly.

But whatever, all this serves essentially as a backdrop to the most crucial elements of Morton Smith's discovery, that there really was a 'secret' element to Jesus's teaching, and a similarly 'secret' version of Mark's gospel, without there being anything heretical or unorthodox about them.

Now by way of qualification, it is important to realise that Clement, who was most likely an Athenian by birth, had been schooled in Greek philosophy as well as Christianity, and therefore had at least some sympathies towards certain aspects of Gnosticism. Unlike any Docetist, however, Clement was quite emphatic that Jesus had been a fully flesh and blood historical figure. As the letter itself makes clear, he was also most strongly opposed to the blatant fabrications apparently being perpetrated by the Gnostic Carpocratians. And not least, he tells us, that Mark's actual autographed copy of the secret version of his gospel was still extant in his adopted city of Alexandria in his (Clement's) own time, a perfectly credible assertion, since for him Mark had lived no further in the past than Charles Dickens for us.

So always assuming that the Clement letter is not some peculiarly cunning modern forgery, we seem then to have from both 'Thomas' and the Clement letter some compelling evidence that Jesus genuinely taught a degree of 'gnosticism' with a small 'g', just as he similarly taught communism with a small 'c'. And if this can be sustained, it would at least go some way to explaining the extraordinary proliferation of the Gnostic heresies within Christian ranks during the early centuries.

But the inevitable question – and one with obvious relevance to the 'Thomas' gospel's alleged sayings of Jesus concerning 'disrobing without being ashamed' and the like – is exactly what construction should be put on the 'secret gospel''s description of Jesus spending all night teaching 'the mystery of the kingdom of God' to a young man wearing only 'a linen cloth over his naked body.' In his letter to Theodore Clement firmly refutes the homosexual innuendo 'naked man with naked man' which the scandal-mongering Carpocratians seem to have slipped into their stolen version of

Mark's secret gospel. But even without this interpolation, such a curious mode of dress/undress, for then as for now, can scarcely do other than raise eyebrows.

Yet in fact, as Morton Smith has been quick to recognise, this very 'secret gospel' element actually seems to explain some more of the most long-standing mysteries peculiar to the canonical version of Mark's gospel, in this instance its account of the strange attire of the otherwise unidentified young man who was apparently with Jesus in the garden of Gethsemane on the night of his arrest. According to canonical Mark:

> A young man who followed him had nothing on but a linen cloth. They caught hold of him, but he left the cloth in their hands and ran away naked.
>
> (Mark 14:51–2)

Without the extra information supplied from Clement of Alexandria's 'secret' version, canonical Mark's cryptic reference to this young man has always seemed most puzzling, with the result that New Testament commentators have often suggested the passage to be an autobiographical insert by Mark himself.

This is not to say that it may not have been the young Mark who was thus attired at the time of Jesus's arrest in Gethsemane, as distinct from the seemingly different individual referred to by Clement of Alexandria. But what was Jesus doing asking any young disciples to come to him dressed in this way? The answer, as Clement's version seems to make clear, is that a linen cloth over a naked body was the required state of dress for anyone being taught 'the mystery of the kingdom of God'. Moreover, in 'secret' Mark we learn the surprising fact that the particular pupil receiving this instruction was a rich young man of Bethany raised from the dead by Jesus, an individual who appears to have been none other than Lazarus, the brother of Martha and Mary of Bethany, whose raising from the dead is otherwise mentioned only in the canonical John gospel.

And this in its turn seems to answer yet further questions. To New Testament scholars it has always seemed curious that only John's gospel, the last and markedly the most esoteric of the canonical four, should have described such a spectacular incident as the raising of Lazarus, with none of the other evangelists apparently having heard of it. As earlier remarked, scholars have often suggested that John perhaps deliberately directed his gospel towards the higher doctrines that Jesus reserved for his disciples and closest initiates, the story of the raising of Lazarus therefore arguably being in this category because of the unequivocally God-like powers it implied for Jesus. Now the inclusion of this story in a version of Mark's gospel apparently intended for 'those who were being perfected' seems positive confirmation of this.

Accordingly, one of the strongest arguments for the authenticity of Morton Smith's 'secret gospel' is the way it explains so many otherwise puzzling features from the canonicals. Yet after all this, one disappointing feature perhaps is that the extra chunk of Mark's gospel with which we seem to have been provided does not in the event give us even an already known saying of Jesus, let alone a new one.

But this is not necessarily too great a cause of disappointment. What we have gained is a reasonable indication that Jesus genuinely did conduct some of his teaching in secret – thereby arguably justifying at least some of the non-canonical sayings from the 'Thomas' gospel. Furthermore we have learned the surprising detail that part of Jesus's instruction course for the 'secret of the kingdom of God' seemed to involve some form of ritual in which the pupil or catechumen came to him naked apart from a linen cloth. Besides explaining the young man in Gethsemane of Mark 14:51-2, the apparent fact of this ritual again evokes and corroborates some of the more surprising sayings of the 'Thomas' gospel.

Now of this ritual Morton Smith has suggested that it was Jesus's particular mode of baptism, an argument which has much to commend it, since although the rite of baptism was undoubtedly practised from Christianity's very earliest years (and Jesus himself received baptism from John the Baptist), the canonical gospels strangely tell us absolutely nothing of Jesus himself ever baptising anyone. So could this very silence in itself be an indication that he did indeed practise this rite, but as an accompaniment to his secret teaching?

Of the mode of dress involved, ultimately there is actually little surprise, since there are plenty of indications that in Christianity's earliest years the baptismal candidate was required to be naked. This is attested, for instance, in Hippolytus's third-century *Apostolic Tradition* [3]. We see Jesus himself fully naked in receiving baptism, as depicted in the earliest catacomb frescoes, in the Ravenna mosaics (Figure 5), and later Greek icons. And even in middle age the Emperor Constantine received his baptism naked as late as the fourth century.

But what of the accompanying linen cloth? Even today a vestige of the use of this seems to survive in Roman Catholic baptisms, during which a white veil may sometimes be placed over the candidate's head. But what is its origin? A curiosity here is that a linen cloth over a naked body was the very apparel Jesus received when laid in the tomb after the Crucifixion. We will recall that according to the lost 'Gospel of the Hebrews' Jesus handed over the very same to the 'high priest's servant' at the time of his resurrection (see page 36). Furthermore it is quite explicit from Paul that Christian baptism was regarded as a form of death prior to rebirth in the spirit. In his first letter to the Colossians, after likening 'the complete stripping of your body' to a form of circumcision, Paul goes on:

> You have been buried with him when you were baptised; and by baptism too you have been raised up with him.
>
> (I Colossians 2:12)

Paul touches on the same theme in his letter to the Romans:

> You have been taught that when we were baptised in Christ Jesus we were baptised in his death; in other words we went into the tomb with him and joined him in death.
>
> (Romans 6:2–3)

Figure 5. Baptism of Jesus, from the Arian Baptistery, Ravenna, circa fifth century.

Not least, we have seen from the 'secret gospel' that the young man/Lazarus who received Jesus's special instruction had undergone what had at least appeared to be death.

So did Jesus's strange ritual in part require the candidate to re-enact the very death that Jesus knew he personally was about to undergo? Clearly there is a great deal more that we simply do not know of what went on during the last days of Jesus's ministry, not least how exactly he fired a group of otherwise very ordinary individuals to go out after his death and found the world religion that today bears his name.

But clearly also we should at the very least no longer rest quite so confidently on the belief that only the canonical gospels provide all of the story that there is to tell.

Chapter 8

Words from Jesus's Brother?

In searching for words of Jesus that are preserved outside the canonical gospels, it can be all too easy to assume that the only worthwhile sources are likely to be obscure tomes tucked away in some dusty library, as in Morton Smith's Mar Saba, or a hidden cache of ancient manuscripts, as found at Nag Hammadi.

Yet could it be that some words of Jesus, though not in the gospels, and unstated and unrecognised as such, have been quite literally always under Christians' noses as part of their ordinary Bibles?

A key document in this context is perhaps the most ignored book in the entire New Testament, the Letter of James, a mere three-thousand word epistle which has long sat virtually unnoticed between the acknowlegedly more impressive and more often quoted missives attributed to Saints Paul and Peter. Martin Luther called the letter 'a right strawy epistle',[1] and because attention is rarely directed to it, even many devout Christians have hardly ever glanced at it.

Yet in its very opening line this letter's author states himself to be 'James, servant of God and of the Lord Jesus Christ'. And for several scholars this absence of any other introduction, plus several other indications, has strongly suggested this individual to have been none other than the James, brother of Jesus and first head of the earliest Christian community, whose pointed neglect by the canonical evangelists we noted in an earlier chapter.

Now it will be recalled that this James, whom both Paul and the 'Hebrews' gospel state to have experienced a special Resurrection appearance by Jesus, was head of that first Jerusalem Jewish-Christian community who, as described in Acts:

> ... all lived together and owned everything in common; they sold

> their goods and possessions and shared out the proceeds among themselves according to what each one needed. They went as a body to the Temple every day but met in their houses for the breaking of bread; they shared their food gladly and generously; they praised God and were looked up to by everyone.
>
> (Acts 2:44–47)

In line with this, the letter in fact gives every indication of having been written at just such a time when Christians were still worshipping within the Jewish religion. For instance, it refers to the synagogue as still the expected place of worship, whereas even before the end of the first century Jews and Christians had gone their separate ways. Furthermore James himself, although quite clearly having accepted the new Christianity, is quite independently referred to as continuing to worship at the Jerusalem Temple with a punctiliousness to the Jewish Law well beyond anything his deceased brother either practised or preached. According to an extract from the second-century historian Hegesippus that has been faithfully preserved by Bishop Eusebius:

> He [James] drank no wine or intoxicating liquor and ate no animal food; no razor came near his head; he did not smear himself with oil, and took no baths. He alone was permitted to enter the Holy Place [of the Jerusalem Temple], for his garments were not of wool but of linen. He used to enter the Sanctuary alone, and was often found on his knees beseeching forgiveness for the people, so that his knees grew hard like a camel's from his continually bending them in worship of God.... [2]

In fact such intense religious observance on James's part would quite likely have contributed to why, in his lifetime, the first Jewish Christian community were, as already noted from Acts, 'looked up to by everyone'. Even so, just like his brother before him, James apparently had enemies within the Jewish high priesthood. From no less an authority than the first-century Jewish historian Josephus we learn that in AD 62 a particularly extreme high priest, Ananus, seized an opportunity to act high-handedly at the time of an interregnum between two Roman procurators. In Josephus's words:

> The younger Ananus ... was headstrong in character and audacious in the extreme. He belonged to the sect of the Sadducees, who in judging offenders are cruel beyond any of the Jews, as I have already made clear. Being a man of this kind Ananus thought he had a convenient opportunity as Festus [the previous Roman procurator] was dead and Albinus [Festus's appointed successor] still on the way. So he assembled a council of judges and brought before it James, the brother of Jesus, known as Christ, and several others, on a charge of breaking the law, and handed them over to be stoned. But those who were considered the most fair-minded people in the City, and strict in their observance of the Law, were most indignant at this, and sent secretly to the king [Herod Agrippa II] imploring him to write to Ananus to stop behaving in this way.[3]

Now unfortunately for James, the intercession of these 'fair-minded people' must have come too late. As recorded in an extract from Hegesippus yet again preserved by Eusebius,[4] James was thrown from the Temple parapet, stoned, and then beaten over the head with a fuller's club. Despite such injustices, James is described as praying for his persecutors to be forgiven even with his dying breath, just as his brother had done from the cross some three decades before.

Accordingly, if we are to believe that the New Testament Letter of James really was written by James brother of Jesus – and New Testament theologian the late Dr John Robinson has been but one of several major scholars to have taken this view[5] – the interesting question arises as to whether this man, with his inevitable intimate knowledge of Jesus, may anywhere in his letter have preserved anything of his brother's actual words?

In fact, according to some authorities at least, we do not have to look very hard for these. As remarked by the New Testament scholar Dr J.H. Moulton, the letter is simply steeped in the very same thinking as that of the author of the Sermon on the Mount. In Moulton's words: 'His [James's] short passages are simply studded with quotations from, or allusions to, the words of Jesus'. [6]

Similarly another writer has stated that although the letter says very little about Jesus - it contains only two mentions of his name - this is simply because it was almost completely made up of his words.[7]

Certainly, when the letter is studied closely, the opening of its second chapter is quite unmistakably indicative of this, revealing a particular closeness to the spirit of what Jesus taught:

> Now suppose a man comes into your synagogue beautifully dressed and with a gold ring, and at the same time a poor man comes in, in shabby clothes, and you take notice of the well-dressed man and say, 'Come this way to the best seats'; then you tell the poor man, 'Stand over there', or 'You can sit on the floor by my foot-rest'. Can't you see that you have used two different standards in your mind, and turned yourselves into judges, and corrupt judges at that?
>
> (James 2:2–4)

Not only does this evoke the Matthew gospel's 'Do not judge, and you will not be judged' (Matthew 7:1), it is similarly reminiscent of Jesus's words when railing against the hypocrisy of the scribes and Pharisees:

> Everything they do is done to attract attention, like wearing broader phylacteries and longer tassels, like wanting to take the place of honour at banquets and the front seats in the synagogues, being greeted obsequiously in the market squares and having people call them Rabbi.
>
> (Matthew 23:5–7)

In some passages in James's letter the imagery strongly evokes that of Jesus, as when James reflects on the power of the tongue:

> Once we put a bit into the horse's mouth, to make it do what we want, we have the whole animal under our control. Or think of ships: no matter how big they are, even if a gale is driving them, the man at the helm can steer them anywhere he likes by controlling a tiny rudder. So is the tongue only a tiny part of the body, but it can proudly claim it does great things. Think how small a flame can set fire to a huge forest; the tongue is a flame like that.
>
> (James 3:3–6)

While other parts of the letter may be said to reflect sayings of Jesus already known from canonical sources, there are certain ones which have no canonical parallel, and arguably these may derive from otherwise unrecorded sayings of Jesus. The following are just a selection:

> Happy is the man who holds out under temptation, for having been tested he will receive the reward of Life, which God has promised to those who love him.
>
> (James 1:12)
>
> You must do what the word tells you, and not just listen to it and deceive yourselves.
>
> (James 1:22)
>
> Does any water supply give a flow of fresh water and salt water out of the same pipe? Can a fig tree give you olives, my brothers, or a vine give figs? No more can sea water give you fresh water.
>
> (James 3:11,12)
>
> You are as unfaithful as adulterous wives; don't you realise that making the world your friend is making God your enemy? Anyone who chooses the world for his friend turns himself into God's enemy.
>
> (James 4:4)

It may of course be unfair to James to rob him of the authorship of anything that even vaguely sounds like his brother. There is no reason to believe why, not least because he was brought up in the very same clearly God-fearing Galilean family as Jesus, he should not have developed in his own right at least something of the same gifts of forthright speech and down-to-earth, countryman-type imagery so notable of his brother.

In fact, quite probably also along with Jesus, James seems to have had a good fluency in Greek, for New Testament scholars are generally agreed that his letter was actually written in this language, even though its author was clearly a Jew. Despite this feature at one time being regarded as one of the biggest obstacles to acceptance of James's authorship, because it was thought most unlikely that a simple Galilean would have had such a command of Greek, now this argument no longer holds much force. As has been remarked by J.N. Sevenster in his 'Do You Know Greek? How Much Greek Could the First Jewish Christians have Known?':

> It has now been clearly demonstrated that a knowledge of Greek was in no way restricted to the upper circles, which were permeated with Jewish culture, but was to be found in all circles of Jewish society, and certainly in places bordering on regions where Greek was much spoken, e.g. Galilee.[8]

So at least in James's letter we have more than a possibility of yet further additions to our store of non-canonical sayings of Jesus. And despite the lack of attention that he and his letter have received on the part of orthodox Christianity, there is every reason to believe that during the first century he may have been a prime source of preserving Jesus's sayings, particularly any not included in the Gentile-inclined canonical sources. After all, he knew Jesus as a member of his own family. He steered the Jerusalem community of Christians for some three decades after his brother's death, ten times longer than the longest estimate of Jesus's own ministry.

Furthermore even after his death the Palestine-based 'family business' that he took over directly from Jesus seems to have been carried on via yet another branch of the family, the grandsons of Jude, brother of Jesus and James, who is mentioned in Mark 6:3 and Matthew 13:55. On these grandsons our old friend Eusebius quoted an interesting passage from the second-century historian Hegesippus:

> And there still survived of the Lord's family the grandsons of Jude, who was said to be his brother, humanly speaking. These were informed against as being of David's line, and brought by the *evocatus* before Domitian Caesar [AD 81–96], who was as afraid of the advent of Christ as Herod had been. Domitian asked them whether they were descended from David, and they admitted it. Then he asked them what property they owned and what funds they had at their disposal. They replied that they only had 9,000 denarii between them, half belonging to each; this, they said, was not available in cash, but was the estimated value of only twenty-

> five acres of land, from which they raised the money to pay their taxes and the wherewithal to support themselves by their own toil.[9]

Eusebius goes on:

> Then, the writer continues, they showed him their hands, putting forward as proof of their toil the hardness of their bodies and the calluses impressed on their hands by incessant labour. When asked about Christ and his Kingdom – what it was like, and where and when it would appear – they explained that it was not of this world or anywhere on earth but angelic and in heaven, and would be established at the end of the world ... On hearing this, Domitian found no fault with them, but despising them as beneath his notice let them go free ... and thanks to the establishment of peace they lived on into Trajan's time.

Clearly these so convincingly rustic great-nephews of Jesus were a long way removed from the markedly Gentile development of what might be termed Christianity proper that was going on, despite enormous obstacles, in Rome and elsewhere at this time. So what source did they have for their so confident assertions about the kingdom that their great-uncle had proclaimed? Was it the lost 'Gospel of the Hebrews' or the equally lost Aramaic 'Sayings' as collected by Matthew? Or did they have their own word-of-mouth tradition? For the present at least, the answer is lost in the mists of history.

Chapter 9

Words from Some Surprising Sources

However surprised we may have been to come across possible words of Jesus in a letter written by his brother, even more surprising is that another albeit limited source of otherwise unrecorded sayings by him is the Hebrew Talmud, the Jewish equivalent of the Christian New Testament.

The Talmud consists of a variety of Jewish rabbinic writings principally comprising first the Mishnah, compiled about AD 200 under the editorship of the great Rabbi Judah the Prince, and second, the Gemara, a commentary on the Mishnah, composed between the third and fifth centuries. The references to Jesus, inclusive of sayings, are to be found in the Mishnah's supplements, the Baraitha and Tosefta.

Now first it needs to be understood that the name under which Jesus appears in these is not 'Jesus' as such – which is a latinisation – but 'Yeshu' ('God saves' in Aramaic), which was a common enough name among Jews of that time.

Also, as indeed might be expected, by no means all the Talmudic references to Jesus are complimentary. A common appellation for him is 'Yeshu Ben Pantera', an allusion to a rumour, widespread among non-Christian Jews during the earliest centuries, that he was the son of an illegitimate union between his mother Miriam, or Mary, and a Roman soldier variously called Pandera, Pantera or Panthera.[1] The Talmud's oldest statement about Jesus is in fact:

> Rabbi Shimeon ben Azzai said, I found a genealogical roll in Jerusalem wherein was recorded, Such-an-one [i.e. Jesus] is a bastard of an adulteress.[2]

While any such question of Jesus's paternity is not one to concern us here, it is at least worth noting that the idea does happen to correspond with the 'Gospel of Thomas''s 105th Saying:

> Jesus said, 'He who knows the father and the mother will be called the son of a harlot'.

Furthermore this in its turn finds some corroboration in the form of a curious remark, 'We were not born of prostitution,' made of Jesus by a group of Jews in John's gospel (8:42). In its bizarre way this represents tacit acknowledgement even among orthodox Jews that there was controversy and uncertainty over the exact circumstances of Jesus's birth.

But with regard to the sayings proper which the Talmud attributes to Jesus, needing stress is the chaotic nature of much Mishnaic material, almost on a par with Christian apocrypha. Some of the words as purportedly spoken by Jesus are indeed quite patently apocryphal. Typical, inclusive of some totally unconvincing sayings attributed to him, is the following episode from the Gemara:

> When king Jannaeus slew our rabbis, Joshua [ben Perachya] and Jesus [Yeshu] went to Alexandria in Egypt. When there was peace Simeon ben Shetah sent for him .... So they (Joshua and Jesus) came, and were treated with much honour at an inn. Joshua said: 'What a pretty woman our hostess is!'. Jesus replied, 'Rabbi, her eyelashes are too short'. Joshua responded: 'You wretch, why do you fill your mind with such ideas?'. He sent out four hundred trumpets and denounced him as accursed. Jesus went to him many times, pleading to be allowed back, but was ignored.
>
> One day Joshua was reciting the *Shema* [The Jewish confession of faith, 'Hear, O Israel' (Deuteronomy 6:4–5)] when Jesus came to him, and Joshua was minded at this time not to send him away. He motioned with his hand that Jesus should wait while he recited the *Shema*, as he did not want to be interrupted. But Jesus, thinking he was turning him away yet again, set up a brick and began worshipping it. Joshua told him, 'Repent!'. To this Jesus responded, 'According to what you have taught me, anyone who sins and encourages others to sin should be given no opportunity to repent'.[3]

Needless to say, not only is the entire setting anachronistic (the

Hasmonean ruler Alexander Jannaeus's suppression of the Pharisees was a hundred years before Jesus's time), but also the described words and actions do not even begin to be convincing of the historical Jesus.

In another Talmudic example a Christian philosopher is set a test question on a matter of property rights between a brother and a sister. He purportedly responds with an otherwise unknown alleged saying of Jesus 'A son and a daughter shall inherit alike.'[4] This again is most suspect, not least because time and again in the canonical gospels Jesus is represented as studiously avoiding becoming involved in any such secular matters. In Luke's gospel, when asked specifically on a matter of inheritance, he responds: 'My friend, who appointed me your judge, or the arbitrator of your claims?' (Luke 12:14). And his parable of the vineyard labourers of Matthew 20:1–16, in which the workers who arrive at the eleventh hour receive exactly the same wages as those who have toiled all day, is a classic instance of his total disregard for any normal standards of economic justice.

But considerably more interesting from the Talmud is a passage relating to Rabbi Eliezer, a Jewish teacher known to have lived in the generation immediately following that of Jesus and his disciples, and to have been somewhat sympathetic towards Christians. Apparently this sympathy brought Eliezer some hostility from his fellow-Jews, which he related to his disciple Rabbi Aqiba as follows:

> Once I was walking along the upper market of Sepphoris and met one [of the disciples of Jesus of Nazareth], who was called Jacob of Kefar Sekanya. He said to me, 'It is written in your Law, "You must not bring the earnings of a prostitute into the house of God"' (Deuteronomy 23:18). So what was to be done with it – a latrine for the High Priest? I did not reply. He said to me, 'Thus Jesus of Nazareth [Yeshu ben Pantera, according to the *Tosefta*] taught me, "For they have been collected with prostitutes' earnings, and prostitutes' earnings they will be again (Micah 1:7); they have come from the gutter, and to the gutter they shall return"'. And the saying pleased me, and because of this I was arrested.[5]

As is clear from other references in Talmudic sources Rabbi Eliezer was an old man in AD 95, the year in which the Roman Emperor Domitian, whose encounter with Jude's grandsons we described in the last chapter, was at his most active in persecuting Christians. So it is perfectly reasonable that earlier in his life Eliezer may well have come across individuals who had directly heard Jesus's words, particularly given that the setting of the story is Sepphoris, Galilee's largest town, which was a mere four miles from Jesus's home village of Nazareth.

Furthermore the earthy robustness of the one hypothetically original saying 'They have come from the gutter, and to the gutter they shall return,' certainly has a ring of the man who said 'Give to Caesar what belongs to Caesar and to God what belongs to God' (Luke 20:25). There is even just the ghost of a possibility – one certainly taken seriously by the highly respected Jewish scholar Dr Joseph Klausner[6] – that the 'Jacob of Kefar Sekanya' who described himself as having been directly taught by Jesus, may have been none other than our now familiar James, brother of Jesus, perhaps on some return visit to his native Galilee.

But even with regard to this the most encouraging Talmudic saying, great caution is needed. The New Testament scholar Joachim Jeremias, Professor at the University of Göttingen, has pointed out that it lacks anything of the deeper meaning so consistent among Jesus's canonical sayings. In Jeremias's words:

> Can we in the light of the gospel tradition really suppose that Jesus (even supposing he had a deeper intention) would have used in his teaching such a theme as the use of the earnings of prostitutes for purposes connected with the Temple? And apart from that, would Jesus have advocated a more liberal attitude to the strict regulations of the Torah on the matter (Deuteronomy 23:18), sanctioning the use of such money at least for the provision of sanitary arrangements in the Temple? Anyone with the slightest acquaintance with the anti-Christian polemic of the early Talmudic period will have no doubt that this saying has been deliberately placed in the mouth of Jesus with the object of discrediting him.[7]

Even so, some of Jeremias's concerns are difficult to sustain. Since the canonical gospels make it clear that Jesus quite shamelessly went out of his way to associate with prostitutes, as in their commonly reported story of his acceptance of massage from 'a woman who had a bad name in the town' (Luke 7:37), there seems little likelihood that Jesus would have had too many qualms about such women's earnings being used for the Temple. In general he seems to have been far more concerned about the money-lending and other pecuniary corruption on the part of those who affected holier-than-thou airs as the Temple's religious leaders. So although the Talmudic quotation is scarcely one that does much to enrich our collection, it remains at least conceivable as a non-canonical saying.

And that, albeit so little, is about as much as can profitably be gleaned from Jewish sacred literature. But while we are still on the subject of unexpected sources of Jesus's sayings, at least some attention should also be allowed to those attributed to Jesus as preserved in an even more unexpected quarter, the Muslim Qur'ān (or Koran).

By way of preliminary explanation, the Qur'ān, in contrast to the more modest claims of the Christian gospels, professes to have been written by none other than the prophet Muhammad himself directly from dictation given to him by God via the angel Gabriel. According to Islamic tradition Gabriel visited Muhammad when the latter was in a trance, some time around the year AD 610. Gabriel ordered Muhammad to 'recite', whereupon when the prophet awoke from his trance he felt as if the entire text of the Qur'ān had somehow become engraved in his heart.

For any non-Muslim casually perusing the Qur'ān it indeed presents a somewhat unordered framework, as if actually written in a state of mind not dissimilar to that inferred in respect of the Gnostics. And not only does it contain a great deal of reference to Old Testament figures such as Joseph, Abraham, and the prophet Moses, Jesus is referred to around twenty times, all markedly without a hint of the animosity so typical of the Talmud. In fact, there is nothing unexpected about this. From the very time of Muhammad Jesus was recognised as an honoured prophet of Islam, although quite emphatically no more than this.

Now even though the Qur'ān was written more than five centuries after Jesus's death it is just conceivable that its author/recipient might have discovered and incorporated in his book authentic information on Jesus that had come to him from some source other than the canonical gospels. And indeed when we study his Jesus references, we find some quite long, directly quoted sayings. The first of these, in a sūra or chapter all about Jesus's mother Mary, are words which the infant Jesus is alleged to have spoken almost immediately after his birth:

> I am the servant of God [Allah]. He has given me the Gospel and ordained me a prophet. His blessing is upon me wherever I go, and He has commanded me to be steadfast in prayer and to give alms to the poor as long as I shall live. He has exhorted me to honour my mother and has purged me of vanity and wickedness. I was blessed on the day I was born, and blessed I shall be on the day of my death; and may peace be upon me on the day when I shall be raised to life.[8]

In a later sūra called 'Battle Array', Jesus is represented as telling the Israelites:

> I am sent forth to you by God to confirm the Torah already revealed and to give news of an apostle that will come after me whose name is Ahmed [an alternative name for Muhammad].[9]

Still later, in a sūra entitled 'The Table', Jesus is represented as involved in a long, three-part conversation between himself, his disciples and God:

> 'Jesus, son of Mary,' said the disciples, 'can God send down to us from heaven a table spread with food?'.
>
> He replied: 'Have fear of God, if you are true believers'.
>
> 'We wish to eat of it,' they said, 'so that we may reassure our hearts and know that what you said to us is true, and that we may be witnesses of it'.
>
> 'Lord,' said Jesus, the son of Mary, 'send to us from heaven a table spread with food, that it may mark a feast for us and for those that

> will come after us: a sign from You. Give us our sustenance. You are the best Giver'.
>
> God replied: 'I am sending one to you. But whoever of you disbelieves hereafter shall be punished as no man has ever been punished'.
>
> Then God will say: 'Jesus, son of Mary, did you ever say to mankind: "Worship me and my mother as gods beside God?"'.
>
> 'Glory to You,' he will answer, 'how could I say that to which I have no right? If I had ever said so, You would have surely known it. You know what is in my mind, but I cannot tell what is in Yours. You alone know what is hidden. I spoke to them of nothing except what you bade me. I said, "Serve God, my Lord and your Lord". I watched over them while living in their midst, and ever since. You took me to You, You Yourself have been watching over them. You are the witness of all things. They are Your own bondsmen: it is for You to punish or to forgive them. You are the Mighty, the Wise One'.[10]

As will be obvious, yet again, as with so much of the Gnostic material we encountered in earlier chapters, these have nothing of the 'feel' of words once spoken by the historical Jesus, whether newborn, resurrected, or otherwise. They are neither more nor less than what Muslims have always claimed them to be, the stuff of revelation, and as such, not the sort of material we are seeking.

There is also outside of the Qur'ān, but still within the Muslim world, an occasional purported saying of Jesus which appears in the *Hadith* or traditional literature of Islam. One, mention of which can be traced in Christian writing no earlier than a work by Levinus Warnerus in 1644, is at least interesting:

> Whoso craves wealth is like a man who drinks sea-water: the more he drinks, the more he increases his thirst, and he ceases not to drink until he perishes.[11]

Whatever the origin of the form of words, the sentiment of this may be said to be true to Jesus. Another of the same genre, traceable well before the twelfth century, is at least true to Jesus's penchant for the contrary and the unexpected:

> He one day walked with his apostles and they passed by the carcase of a dog. The apostles said, 'How foul is the smell of this dog!'. But Jesus said, 'How white are its teeth!'.[12]

But perhaps the most intriguing of all is an Arabic inscription on the gateway of the great Mosque at Fateh-pur-Sikri, commemorating the triumphal return of the great Moghul Emperor Akbar to his former capital city in the year 1601. This reads:

> Jesus, on whom be peace, has said: 'This world is a bridge. Pass over it. But build not your dwelling there'.[13]

There is absolutely no justification for this being authentic, not least because of its totally unknown origins before 1601, and the fact that there is no other known allusion by Jesus to any bridge. But nonetheless it is so true to Jesus's spirit that we can confidently believe he would have agreed with it.

Chapter 10

Did Jesus Write a Letter?

At the beginning of this book it was stated that, with the exception of scrawling in the dust during the adulterous woman episode, Jesus is not known ever to have committed anything to writing. Nonetheless, deserving of at least some discussion is the fact of a widespread belief during Christianity's early centuries that Jesus did write or at least dictate a letter in response to a written request from a sick king for him to come to his city to cure him of an otherwise incurable disease.

Perhaps predictably, one of our prime sources for this story is the *History of the Church* written by our old friend Bishop Eusebius of Caesarea. And characteristically Eusebius has not failed to provide us with some interesting details of this alleged correspondence, including full transcripts of the texts of the purported letters (although in this instance there are plenty of alternative sources). The basis of the story is that the king who wrote to Jesus was Abgar of Edessa (a small town that is today Urfa in eastern Turkey). And quite incontrovertibly in Jesus's time, when Edessa was a buffer state lying between the Roman and Parthian Empires, the ruler was an Abgar V, who reigned from AD 13 to 50.

Now according to Eusebius, Abgar's letter, as delivered to Jesus in Jerusalem by a courier called Ananias, read as follows:

> Abgar Ukkama, the Toparch, to Jesus the good Saviour who has appeared in the district of Jerusalem – greeting.
>
> I have heard concerning you and your cures, how they are accomplished by you without drugs and herbs. For, as the story goes, you make the blind recover their sight, the lame walk, and you cleanse lepers, and cast out unclean spirits and demons, and you cure those who are tortured by long disease and you raise dead

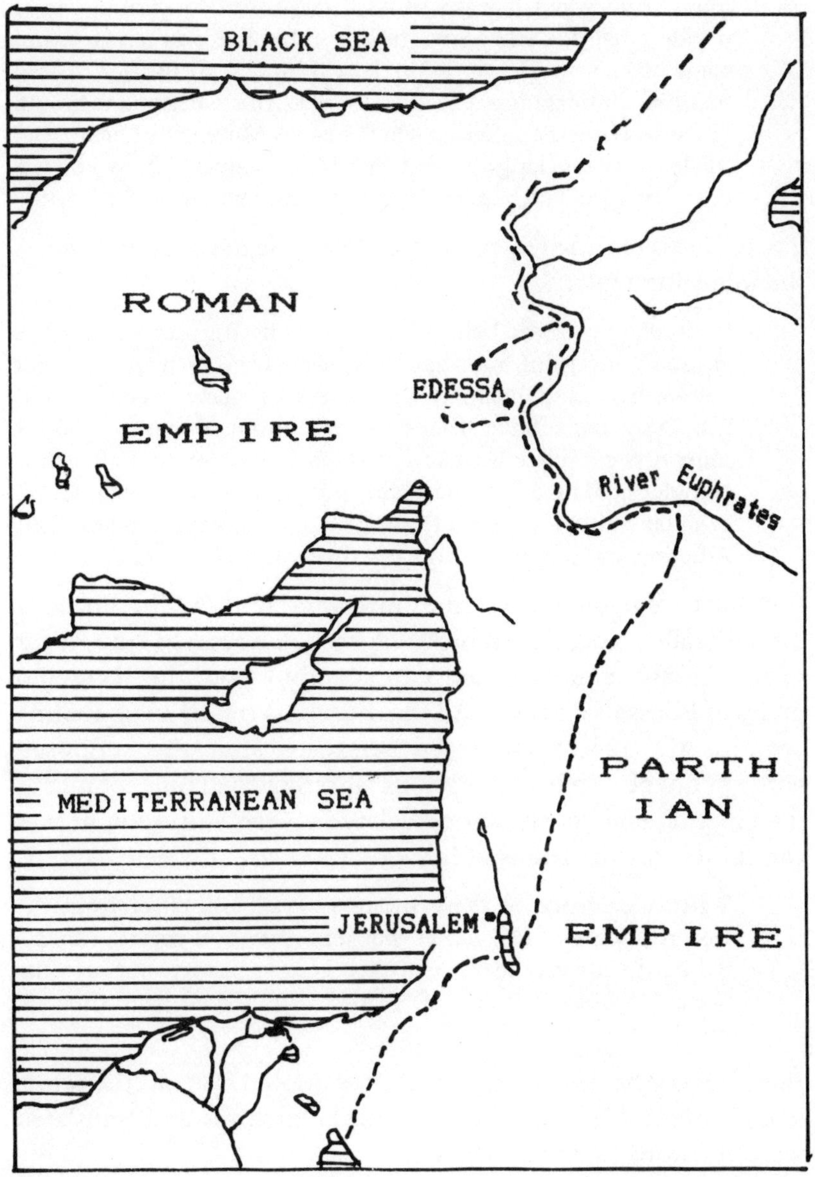

Figure 6. Map of Edessa, showing the political boundaries as they existed in Jesus's time.

> men. And when I heard of all these things concerning you I decided that it is one or two things, either that you are God and came down from Heaven to do these things, or are the Son of God for doing these things. For this reason I write to beg you to hasten to me and heal the suffering which I have. Moreoever I heard that the Jews are mocking you and wish to ill-treat you. Now I have a city very small and venerable which is enough for both of us.[1]

To this Jesus reputedly sent back to Abgar via the courier Ananias the following reply:

> Blessed are you who believed in me, not having seen me, for it is written concerning me that those who have seen me will not believe in me, and that those who have not seen me will believe and live. Now concerning what you wrote to me, to come to you, I must first complete here all for which I was sent, and after thus completing it be taken up to Him who sent me, and when I have been taken up, I will send to you one of my disciples to heal your suffering and give life to you and those with you.

Eusebius went on to describe how after Jesus's Crucifixion a disciple called Thaddaeus, or Addai, visited Edessa to cure Abgar of his disease, and preached Christianity before the King and many of Edessa's citizens. All this Eusebius set down on writing around AD 325, some three centuries after the supposed correspondence, so it was nearly as far removed in time for him as the Great Plague for us. Nonetheless as a good historian he was careful to provide details of his sources:

> Written evidence of these things is available, taken from the Record Office of Edessa, at that time the royal capital. In the public documents there, embracing early history and also the events of Abgar's time, this record is preserved from then till now.[2]

Furthermore he described what he had quoted from as 'the actual letters, which I have extracted from the archives and translated word for word from the Syriac'.[3]

At face value this is quite definitely impressive, for certainly the archive office at Edessa had an excellent reputation in the early centuries – an early Syriac chronicle remarking: 'The archives of

Edessa ... err in nothing, and ... make everything known to us truly'.[4]

And since the language of Edessa was Syriac, virtually the same as that spoken by Jesus and his disciples, there can be little doubting that it would have been easy enough for Jesus and Abgar to exchange correspondence with each other. Edessa in fact became the prime centre for the Syriac language during subsequent centuries.

Nonetheless there is something distinctly unconvincing about Jesus's purported reply, harking as it does to the resurrected Jesus's words to Doubting Thomas as preserved in John 20:19: 'You believe because you can see me. Happy are those who have not seen and yet believe'.

One of the give-aways is the remark 'it is written', for theoretically those words should not have been either 'written' or even yet spoken at the time of the letter's composition, if it genuinely did emanate from Jesus's lifetime.

Accordingly some serious questions need to be raised as to the precise nature of the documents which Eusebius said were kept at Edessa, exactly how ancient they might have been, and whether Eusebius ever actually studied them directly.

First, it is important to note that besides Eusebius's account there are other early documents relating the story of the correspondence, one of the most important of which is the Syriac *Acts of Thaddaeus* preserved in a sixth-century manuscript in the British Museum.[5] Although this does not include the full texts of the letters, and is much more fragmentary than a substantially fuller version, *The Doctrine of Addai*, preserved in Leningrad,[6] it does include the important passage:

> You have in written documents the evidence of these things, which is taken from the Book of Records which is at Edessa; for at that time the kingdom was still standing. In the public documents, therefore, that are there, in which is contained whatever has been done by those of old up to the time of Abgar, these things also are found preserved there up to the present hour.[7]

As will be observed, this is so like Eusebius's statement that there has to be a suspicion that he drew his information from a copy of this, or more likely some closely-related document, rather than from any originals in the Edessa archives. Furthermore the remark that 'at that time the kingdom was still standing' relates to the fact that between AD 212 and 216 the Romans extinguished the line of Abgars and Manus who up to that time had successively ruled Edessa, reducing it instead to the status of a military *colonia*. This indicates that whoever wrote the *Acts of Thaddaeus* must have written his account sometime after the Roman takeover. As for the Leningrad *Doctrine of Addai*, which does include a slightly differing text of the letters, this shows every sign of late fourth-century composition.[8]

While all this might look very black as to there ever having been any genuine correspondence between Jesus and Abgar V, nonetheless the whole highly complex set of traditions relating to Edessa's early Christian links do not deserve to be dismissed quite so easily. Quite unquestionably one of the Abgar dynasty, Abgar VIII (the Great), who reigned between AD 177 and 212, did take a very special interest in Christianity. We know that at least as early as his reign a Christian church was built at Edessa, since the near-contemporary *Chronicle of Edessa* records in its entry for the year AD 201, that 'the nave of the church of the Christians was damaged during a severe flood which destroyed the royal palace and drowned two thousand of Edessa's citizens'.[9] Although the remark 'of the Christians' suggests that the chronicle writer was still pagan, it is nonetheless evident that this church must have been officially recognised and tolerated. And even on its own the reference represents the earliest known mention of a purpose-built Christian church in the entire history of Christianity.

In addition several prominent, though not always fully orthodox, Christian writers certainly flourished in Edessa during Abgar VIII's reign, apparently in an atmosphere of ready toleration. One of these was the astrologically-inclined Bardaisan, who tended towards the further reaches of Gnostic heresy; another was

Tatian, who produced a synthesis of the four canonical gospels known as the *Diatessaron*.

Furthermore something peculiar arises when we study Abgar VIII's coinage.[10] Early in his reign, after he had acknowledged the suzerainty of the Roman empire, Abgar VIII adopted a not uncommon custom of portraying the reigning Roman emperor's head on the obverse of Edessa's coinage, with his own portrait deferentially on the reverse. And in the first examples of this the distinctive tiara characteristic of Edessan royal headgear can be seen to be quite plain, as in Figure 7 below.

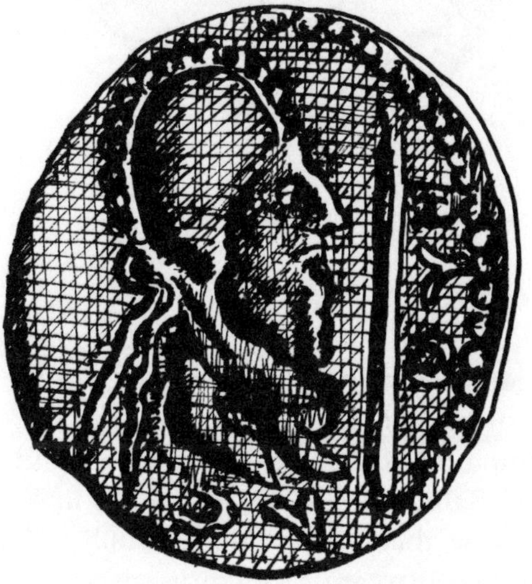

Figure 7. Coin of Abgar VIII of Edessa, showing conventional plain tiara.

But then there came a phase in which the reigning Roman Emperor Commodus fell strongly under the influence of his wife Marcia, who was sympathetic to Christianity, and Christians throughout the Empire enjoyed a welcome spell of tolerance. At this point Abgar's coin portraits can be seen to undergo a significant change, beginning to feature a quite unmistakable jewelled cross on the tiara (Figure 8 overleaf).

Figure 8. Coin of Abgar VIII of Edessa, showing apparent Christian cross on tiara.

Subsequently, when Commodus was succeeded by Septimius Severus, Abgar seems to have become more careful again, sometimes featuring himself with an unadorned tiara, occasionally with a cross, but more commonly with crescent and stars (was this the influence of Bardaisan?), accompanied by up to three crosses. These seem to be the earliest ever examples of any monarch anywhere in the world wearing the Christian cross on his tiara, and seem to indicate that even if Abgar VIII was perhaps not fully a Christian in the modern sense, he was about as near to it as makes little difference.

And adding fuel to the idea that something dramatic happened very early on in Edessa, arguably even before Abgar VIII's reign, is the special status that the city subsequently commanded as a 'holy' place for hermits and pilgrims. During the fourth and fifth centuries hermits clustered in the innumerable caves in the hillside surrounding Edessa. A prince is supposed to have given up the comforts of a palace to become a beggar in the doorways of its churches.[11] And pilgrims flocked to it.

One of these latter was the highly intelligent and observant late fourth-century abbess Egeria or Etheria who devoted three days to Edessa as part of an itinerary that also included Jerusalem and the Sinai. Although Egeria's home seems to have been in far-off Aquitaine, her account of her travels makes clear that she had already known of the Jesus-Abgar correspondence, to the extent of even possessing copies of it. In a vivid description of her visit to Edessa,[12] she recounted being given a conducted tour by the city's bishop, who took her to the shrine where the body of the apostle Thomas had recently been brought and given its last resting place, after having earlier been brought from India. Here Egeria reported listening to readings 'from the writings of holy Thomas himself'. Fascinatingly, these readings must almost certainly have been from a copy of our now familiar Oxyrhynchus/ Nag Hammadi 'Gospel of Thomas', which some scholars believe actually to have been composed in Edessa.[13]

But still the high point of interest seemed to be the letter correspondence. Egeria was shown both the former royal palace and a 'huge marble portrait' of Abgar (theoretically the one contemporary with Jesus), and told glowingly 'Before he saw the Lord he believed in him as the true son of God', a clear reference to the words of Jesus's alleged letter. She was further informed that the letter gave Edessa special protection - by her time it seems to have acquired an extra sentence, 'And your city shall be blessed and no enemy shall ever be master of it again' – and both Abgar's letter to Jesus and Jesus's to Abgar were read to her from the gate by which Abgar's messenger Ananias was supposed to have returned from his visit to Jesus. She was then given copies of both letters, despite her already remarked admission, 'I have copies of them at home'.

So what are we to make of the letters and the story surrounding them? Was there ever any genuine correspondence between Jesus and Abgar V? Or was the story of this and accompanying letters perhaps 'invented' some time in the reign of Abgar VIII? Whatever the truth behind it all, in the sixth century interest in the letters became almost completely eclipsed by the discovery, apparently in a hiding place above one of Edessa's gates, of the reputedly miraculous imprint of Jesus on cloth that became known as the Image of Edessa, or Holy Mandylion. Virtually overnight this took over Jesus's letter's former role as a magical protection agent, being credited with saving the city from the Persians in AD 544.

Exactly four centuries later Jesus's letter is heard of again, brought from Edessa to Constantinople along with the cloth image when this latter was triumphantly transferred to the Imperial relic collection.[14] But as a purported relic it was totally overshadowed by the Image, and clearly of questionable authenticity even to the Byzantines, for another copy, also supposed to be the original, was transferred to Constantinople in 1032. In 1185 one or other of these appears to have been stolen, along with its reliquary, when a mob broke into the Imperial Chapel in Constantinople.

Ultimately all that can be said with any certainty is that Edessa would genuinely seem to have received Christian evangelism very early. The difficult question is exactly how early. The answer lies somewhere locked in the origins of the widespread but all too often adulterated versions of the Abgar story, and whatever still unexcavated remains of Edessa's Christian past may slumber beneath the overwhelmingly Turkish Muslim town of Urfa that now covers the site.

But even if the letter correspondence really offers nothing to add to any collection of non-canonical genuine words of Jesus, nonetheless tucked away in the rest of the Abgar story is one further purported saying that just may have a crucial spark of authenticity. As we have already remarked, the *Doctrine of Addai*, the Leningrad manuscript, which contains the fullest account of the Abgar story, shows many signs of adulterations and interpolations datable up to and including the fourth century AD. But it does include one interesting passage relating to the death of Addai or Thaddaeus, the disciple reputed to have cured Abgar of his disease and brought Christianity to Edessa. When the citizens hear that Addai is dying (apparently of natural causes), they send to him 'honourable and costly garments, in which he should be buried'. But Addai refuses them with the words:

> Never in my life have I taken anything from you, and I will not compromise those words which Christ taught me: "Accept not anything from any man, and do not own anything in this world".[15]

Now although these words have no ready parallel in any canonical gospel, they have Jesus's simplicity and directness of style, and are totally in the spirit of his instructions to his disciples when, as described in Matthew's gospel, he sent them out on their works of healing:

> You received without charge, give without charge. Provide yourselves with no gold or silver, not even with a few coppers for your purses, with no haversack for the journey, or spare tunic or footwear or a staff, for the workman deserves his keep.
>
> (Matthew 10:8–10)

So it is all a lesson that even the most apocryphal of stories may contain more than a kernel of truth. And although the extant store of *possibly* authentic words of Jesus is becoming ever more depleted, even yet it is still not quite exhausted.

Chapter 11

A Few More Words?

In December 1905, when still working among the rubbish heaps at Oxyrhynchus, Grenfell and Hunt came across a scorched, worm-eaten fragment measuring no more than 8.8 by 7.4 centimetres ($3^1/_2$ x 3 inches) bearing 45 lines in a microscopic Greek script that seems to have come from a miniature book of gospels designed for use as an amulet. That sacred books were miniaturised for such purposes is known from the writings of the fourth-century Bishop of Constantinople, St John Chrysostom, who remarked in one of his sermons that 'women and little children are in the habit of wearing gospel books round their necks in place of a large amulet'. [1]

The interesting feature of this particular scrap is that the writing, although so tiny, is readily legible and datable to around AD 400. Furthermore, as in the case of Egerton Papyrus 2, it seems to derive from an otherwise unknown gospel. The first seven lines are thought to come from the end of a discourse by Jesus with his disciples on the way to the Temple, and consist of three sentences of which only one can be read with certainty:

> First, before he does wrong [?], he uses every artifice. But be careful, in case you also suffer in the same way as they. For not only in life [?] do wrong-doers receive human chastisement, they must also suffer punishment and great torment.[2]

Although this seems to offer nothing particularly new or startling, there then follows an otherwise quite unknown story about Jesus, including further reputed sayings:

> And he took them with him into the very place of purity and walked into the Temple. And a certain Pharisee, a chief priest, Levi by name, came to meet them and said to the Saviour,
>
> 'Who permitted you to walk upon this place of purity and look

upon these holy vessels, when you have not first washed and your disciples have not washed their feet? But you have walked on this sacred spot in a state of defilement, this clean place, on which no one can walk unless he has washed and has changed his clothes, nor can he venture to look upon these holy vessels'.

The Saviour stopped with his disciples and answered,

'Since you are in the Temple, are you clean?'.

He says to him,

'I am clean; for I have washed in the pool of David and I went down to it by one ladder and up by another, and I have put on clean white clothing, and then I came and looked at these holy vessels'.

The Saviour answered and said to him,

'Woe to the blind who do not see! You have washed in these waters poured forth, in which dogs and swine lie night and day; and you have washed and scoured your outside skin, which harlots and flute girls anoint and wash and scour and beautify to arouse men's lust, though inwardly it is full of scorpions, and all unrighteousness. But I and my [disciples], whom you call unwashed, we have bathed in living waters [...] which have come from [...] But woe to the ...'.[3]

Scholarly opinions on this scrap have been sharply divided. When it was first published in 1907 Göttingen University's Professor Emil Schürer, author of the monumental seven volume *A History of the Jewish People in the Time of Jesus Christ*, roundly dismissed it as worthless on the grounds of the writer's apparent appalling ignorance on matters of Jewish ritual in the period contemporary with Jesus.[4] Many others supported him, and this view has carried even to the present day.[5] It has seemed most unlikely for laymen to have been allowed to view the Temple's sacred vessels. No 'pool of David' is known ever to have existed within the Temple precincts, and the idea of a Jewish chief priest cleansing himself by day in the same water which dogs and pigs use by night has been thought so absurd as to be laughable.

But the scrap's authenticity has more recently been stoutly defended by a successor of Schürer's at Göttingen, Professor Joachim

Jeremias.[6] Jeremias has pointed out that the sacred vessels mentioned were more likely to have been in storechambers surrounding the Temple forecourt, and these would have been accessible to ordinary laity. During the early 1930s archaeological excavations revealed the existence of huge twin pools just a hundred yards to the north of the Temple, one of which could easily have been called the 'pool of David'. The reference to 'dogs and swine' Jeremias has interpreted as a figurative allusion to unclean human beings, as in Matthew 7:6.

And Jeremias has even gone further to suggest that since the phrase 'harlots and flute girls' is unknown from any canonical gospel, but occurs in a known extract from the 'Gospel of the Hebrews' [7], the scrap may actually be from that gospel. In support of this view is the fact that the fragment exhibits a confidence in speaking of Jewish ritual quite untypical of the normal run of apocrypha. It seems to satisfy the characteristics of Jesus we identified in Chapter 2, and it shows not the slightest trace of Gnosticism.

Nor have we exhausted the occurrence of yet more occasional non-canonical sayings of Jesus in the preserved writings of Church fathers and others from the centuries immediately following Jesus's Crucifixion, just as we noted in the last chapter in respect of the *Doctrine of Addai.*

To St Clement of Rome, for instance, who was head of the Roman Church about the end of the first century AD, have been attributed two surviving epistles that were so highly regarded in the early centuries that they were included in the fifth-century Codex Alexandrinus, one of the great manuscripts on which our present-day Bibles have been based. Modern scholars are only prepared to accept the first epistle as genuinely of Clement's authorship, but both are unquestionably early and both contain reputed sayings of Jesus of at least marginal interest.

In the first epistle, written in an attempt to defuse fierce squabbling that had broken out among the Christians of Corinth, Clement pleaded for tolerance and patience with the words:

> Most of all remembering the words spoken by the Lord Jesus ... for he said: 'Have mercy, that you may receive mercy. Forgive, that you in your turn may be forgiven. Do to others nothing that you would not wish them to do to you. Whatever you give to others, so will you receive. Whatever judgement you make, so will you be judged. Whatever kindness you do, so you will receive kindness. Whatever measure you mete out, so it will be measured out to you'.[8]

Although this is of course merely something of a synthesis of Jesus's well-known teachings from the Sermon on the Mount, that Jesus may conceivably have used a specific formula of this kind is independently suggested by a very similar saying preserved from the writings of the early second-century Christian martyr Polycarp. Polycarp claimed in his youth to have talked to John, author of the Fourth Gospel, and according to his version of the saying, Jesus taught:

> Do not judge, so that you may not be judged; forgive, and you will be forgiven; show mercy, so that you may receive mercy; whatever measure you use, so it will be measured back to you; and blessed are the poor, for the kingdom of God belongs to them.[9]

The Second Epistle attributed to St Clement, although no longer seriously thought to have been written by him (it was more probably by a late second-century Bishop of Rome called Soter), actually contains substantially more non-canonical sayings:

> For he said: 'Not everyone who says to me, "Lord, Lord," will be saved, but only he whose acts are in accord with righteousness'.
>
> The Lord said: 'Even though you may be a bosom companion, if you do not follow my commandments I will turn you away, saying, "Leave me. I do not know where you have come from, you evil-doer"'.
>
> For the Lord said in the gospel, 'If you do not look after the small things, why should you receive anything bigger? For I tell you, he who is faithful in the smallest things, is also faithful in the greatest'.
>
> For the Lord said, 'Be like lambs in the midst of wolves'. But Peter

> replied, 'What if the wolves savage the lambs?', Jesus said to Peter, 'The lambs will have no fear of the wolves after they are dead. You also should have no fear of anyone who although he may kill you, has no other power over you. Rather be afraid of Him who, after you are dead, has the power over your soul and body to cast them into hellfire'.

> For the Lord himself, when asked by someone when his kingdom would come, said, 'When the two shall be one, and the outside as the inside, and the male with the female neither male or female'.[10]

Disappointingly, there is very little of startling interest here. All except the last have at least some form of basis in sayings from the canonical gospels, and may simply be rather loose quotations from these. The last is already familiar to us from the 'Gospel of Thomas' (see page 63), and perhaps the most valuable feature of it is its indication that in the second century at least some form of this gospel was still being accepted in the highest Christian circles.

Just as Clement's epistles were found as part of the fifth-century Bible manuscript known as the Codex Alexandrinus, so, when during the last century the German scholar Constantin Tischendorf made his momentous find of the Codex Sinaiticus at St Catherine's Monastery in the Sinai desert, among the latter's pages came to light the complete text of a very anti-Jewish letter known as the 'Epistle of Barnabas'.[11] Modern scholars mostly doubt the traditional attribution of this to the Barnabas described as Paul's companion in Acts, but nonetheless it is generally recognised as having been written some time between AD 70 and the end of the first century AD. Furthermore it does have a non-canonical saying worthy of at least some consideration:

> Thus he said, 'Those who want to see me, and to reach my kingdom, must gain hold on me via tribulation and suffering'.
> ('Epistle' 7:11)

This happens to echo a remark of Paul and Barnabas when preaching in Antioch after they had been stoned on a mission to Lyaonia:

> We all have to experience many hardships ... before we enter the

kingdom of God.

(Acts 14:22)

But more pertinently perhaps, it also has a parallel in a very early Christian manual of morals and Church practice known as the Didache, an eleventh-century copy of which was discovered in a Constantinople library in 1873. Among various admonitions which sound like Jesus in the Didache (although they are not directly attributed to him), there is one that parallels Barnabas, with the words:

> Welcome any accidents that happen to you as good, knowing that nothing is done without God.[12]

The New Testament scholar Resch, one of the pioneers of interest in non-canonical sayings, thought this passage had a particularly good claim to authenticity.

Another non-canonical reputed saying, known from about twenty separate sources, including the famous Justin Martyr,[13] is:

> In whatsoever things I apprehend you, in these I shall judge you.

Despite the somewhat obscure wording, the very frequency with which this recurs among well-respected early Christian writers suggests it has a genuine base in something Jesus once said, its meaning seems to be that individuals will be judged not so much on past misdeeds, as on whatever the state of their soul at the time they die. In other words, a genuinely repentant evil-doer may be worth more than a good man who has lapsed into sin and has died unreconciled to God. It also evokes a recurrent theme of Jesus, that of the need for the soul to be always ready for whatever time death may strike, as in the Parable of the Rich Fool of Luke 12:16–21 (see below, p.139).

Also of at least passing interest are the remains of a single leaf from an unidentified gospel found with some two thousand fragments of a sixth-century Coptic papyrus of the apocryphal 'Acts of Paul' which the New Testament scholar C. Schmidt pieced together in 1904. Translated from the Coptic the first side of the leaf reads:

> ... the doings ... they were awestruck and deeply puzzled. He asked them, 'Why are you so astonished that I can raise the dead, or help the lame to walk, or cure lepers, or heal the sick? Or that I have helped the paralysed and the possessed? Or that I have broken a few loaves and fed whole crowds? Or that I have walked on the sea? Or that I have controlled tempests? If you really believe this and are convinced, then you are very worthy: for truly, if you say to this mountain, throw yourself into the sea, without having any doubt in your mind, then it will happen ...'. One of those who was convinced was called Simon. He said, 'Lord, your doings are truly wonderful. For we have never before seen or heard ...'.

On the second side is found:

> ... ever anyone raised the dead, except you. The Lord told him: 'You will pray for those deeds which I shall do ... But the others I will carry out immediately. These I perform as a temporary means of salvation, wherever they occur, to aid faith in Him who sent me'. Simon said to him, 'Lord, permit me to speak'. He replied: 'Speak, Peter,' for from that time on he addressed them each by name. He said: 'What work can be greater than these ... except raising the dead, and feeding such huge crowds?'. The Lord said to him: 'There are some things even greater than this, and happy are those who have wholeheartedly believed'. But Philip raised his voice angrily, saying, 'What sort of teaching is this?'. But he told him: 'You ...'.[14]

The only non-canonical element in this fragment is its reference to Philip being angry, a tendency which he also exhibits in the apocryphal 'Acts of Philip'. Whatever may be the origins of this still intriguing isolated scrap, it provides nothing of any significance in the way of any hitherto unknown saying of Jesus.

Finally from subsequent centuries there are a few other claimed sayings, though now with markedly dwindling claims to authenticity. Perhaps the only one worth quoting is one which ought at least to appeal to animal lovers. According to this text:

> The Lord [i.e. Jesus] left the city and began walking in the mountains with his disciples. And at one mountain, the approach road of which was steep, they came across a man with a pack-mule. The animal had fallen because of the weight of its load, and the

> man was beating it until it bled. On coming upon him, Jesus asked, 'Sir, why are you hitting your animal? Can you not see that it is too weak for the load? And do you not realise that it's suffering pain?'. But the man replied: 'What business is it of yours? I can beat it as much as I like, because I own it and I paid a lot of money for it. Ask your companions: they know me, and know all about it'. And some of the disciples said, 'Yes, Lord, it is as he says. We saw him buy it'. But the Lord said, 'Don't you notice how much it's bleeding, nor hear its cries of pain?'. And the Lord was sad, and said, 'May you be punished that you are so deaf to its calls to the heavenly Creator, and its cries for mercy. But may there be three times as much retribution for the one of whom it complains and cries in its distress'. He approached and touched the animal, and it got up, its wounds healed. And Jesus said to the man, 'Now go on your way, and don't beat it any more, so that you may receive similar forgiveness'.[15]

The provenance of this tale is one of the weakest. A German writer called Julius Boehmer purportedly learned it from an earlier writer who had apparently died before revealing its exact source, except that it came from a Coptic Bible manuscript in the Paris Library. At least the simplicity of the story gives it rather more of a ring of authenticity than many apocrypha, and Jesus's concern for animals is certainly implied by his canonical remark that not even a sparrow 'falls to the ground without your Father knowing' (Matthew 10:30). But it is anyone's guess whether something of this kind genuinely happened during Jesus's earthly existence, or whether it is just yet another pious fable.

Chapter 12

Words Yet to be Found?

Overall, while we have discovered that a variety of sources offer us sayings of Jesus not directly represented in the canonical gospels, nonetheless a serious question that arises is: What have we gained? The blunt, and perhaps somewhat disappointing answer is: Not a lot. While we may have a few new words of Jesus, and odd curious new episodes in his life, such as the Resurrection appearance to James, these have added little, if anything, to our understanding of the message of Jesus. There are quite a few purported sayings from the Nag Hammadi 'Gospel of Thomas' that we have not considered, and for the reader's further study these are included with others in the Appendix of Documents at the end of this book. Yet further scholarly work is needed to sift what may be uniquely recorded genuine sayings of Jesus from the adulterations of heretic Gnostics.

Both in respect of 'Thomas' and the Mar Saba 'Secret Gospel' perhaps one of the most curious and still incompletely resolved features we have come across is Jesus's apparent advocacy of having no shame for the naked body. But it is important to make clear that if this was indeed a message omitted from the canonical gospels (and some doubts on both 'Thomas' and the 'Secret Gospel' still remain), it was neither a ratification of any naturist exhibitionism, nor, despite the Carpocratians, for sexual licentiousness. The most reasonable construction is that Jesus, as the second Adam, was for his Kingdom of God harking back to humankind's pre-Fall state. If Jesus indeed expected his followers to give up absolutely everything of this world for the Kingdom of God – and time and time again the canonical gospels emphasise this, just as Jesus reiterated it with the manner of his death – then there could have been no more powerful way of symbolising this than by the candidate for the kingdom of God being admitted in the very same state in which he had entered this earthly world. We have already noted how nudity was commonplace even for adults in the earliest Christian baptisms. Only later more prudish eras relinquished the custom.

But aside from offbeat elements such as this, essentially what we have learned from the sprinkling of apparent 'new' words of Jesus that we have come across is that they add very little, if anything at all, to Jesus's words as we have always had them from the canonical gospels. What Jesus taught was nothing that could be straightforwardly codified from one to ten, like Moses's original Ten Commandments. Hence for Jesus there could not be and never can be any hypothetical vital Eleventh Commandment that the surviving documents have somehow missed.

Instead what we have, and always have had, of Jesus is rather like a hologram: even if it were smashed to pieces and individual fragments lost, those that remained would still convey the picture of the whole. While the 'Gospel of Thomas' may have given us a new parable (Sayings 97, 98) relating to the folly of hoarding possessions, it adds nothing to the so-powerful lesson of the Luke gospel's so typically agricultural parable of the Rich Fool:

> There was once a rich man who, having had a good harvest from his land, thought to himself, 'What am I to do? I have not enough room to store my crops'. Then he said, 'This is what I will do: I will pull down my barn and build bigger ones, and store all my grain and my goods in them, and I will say to my soul: My soul, you have plenty of good things laid by for many years to come, take things easy, eat, drink, have a good time'. But God said to him, 'Fool! This very night the demand will be made for your soul; and this hoard of yours, whose will it be then?'.
>
> (Luke 12:16–20)

Similarly the Parable of the Prodigal Son, the Parable of the Good Samaritan, the imprecation to love your enemy, and the refusal to condemn the adulterous woman: all these are mere variants on another theme that is and always has been so singularly Jesus's: the appeal to an unashamedly naked Love that is beyond all human justice and human values.

But just as some quirk of fate brought into our canonical New Testament the story of Jesus and the adulterous woman, an unquestionably authentic story that we would have been greatly the poorer without, so there may yet be new documentary discoveries to be made that could genuinely further enrich our knowledge of Jesus.

Pride among these must be the possibility of one day finding a complete copy, preferably in its original Aramaic, of the very 'Gospel of the Hebrews' from which the adulterous woman story seems to have come, a gospel to which we have so frequently alluded in the course of this book.

Just as the Matthew, Mark, Luke and John gospels were each written as *the* gospels for individual communities during Christianity's formative years, so the 'Gospel of the Hebrews' would quite definitely seem to have been *the* gospel for those Jewish Christians who gathered around Jesus's so undervalued brother James in Jerusalem. Around AD 70, when James had been dead a few years, and the entire Jewish world was shattered by its unsuccessful revolt against the Romans, these Jewish Christians were reported to have headed to Pella on the east bank of the Jordan. As noted earlier, a memory of their existence seems to have been preserved for a few subsequent centuries in the form of occasional references to 'Nazarenes' and 'Ebionites', who were said to be still using the 'Gospel of the Hebrews' at least up to the fourth century AD.

In this regard, that remains of both such a community and their writing may yet be found is indicated by the fact that in 1967, during excavations of the West Church at Pella, a sarcophagus was found beneath the church's apse.[1] From the sarcophagus's Jewish style of decoration and Christian context it is quite evident that it must once have contained the bones of one of the earliest leaders of the community that settled at Pella. It is even conceivable that the original occupant could have been James himself, his bones specially brought from Jerusalem, just as Moses and the Israelites carried the remains of Joseph on their flight out of Egypt,

Figure 9. Sarcophagus of an early Jewish-Christian religious leader, as found at Pella in Jordan.

as described in Exodus 13:19.

Accordingly it is by no means impossible that some day a crucial sealed hoard of manuscripts from a group of this kind could come to light from a hiding-place in or around Pella, just as happened both at Nag Hammadi, and in the case of the Dead Sea Scrolls. Besides the 'Gospel of the Hebrews', quite conceivably such a hoard could contain a copy of the original Aramaic sayings of Jesus, as collected by Jesus's disciple Matthew; perhaps also the hypothetical 'Q' manuscript that scholars believe to have been a source for both Matthew and Luke; perhaps other lost Aramaic writings that as yet we can no more than guess at. The implications and interest-value for Christianity would be far, far greater than anything found at Nag Hammadi.

Inevitably another most profoundly important manuscript find would be that of a full text of the alleged 'Secret Gospel' of Mark. Given the 'secret' nature of this, there are likely never to have been more than a few copies, and since the original was said to have been in Alexandria, Egypt is the most likely location for any that might come to light. Allied to this, of little less import would be discovery of the original letter of Clement of Alexandria from which a still unknown eighteenth-century monk of Mar Saba made the book-extract copy which so astounded Professor Morton Smith. Such a find would effectively put to rest any remaining doubts concerning the validity of Professor Morton Smith's discovery.

Of interest in this context is the fact that there are many caves in the desert surrounding the Mar Saba monastery. In centuries past these were used as homes by hermits, and sometimes by the monks as places of refuge, and Smith was told that vestiges of manuscripts had been found in some of these. He also learned that on one occasion the monk in charge of the monastery's treasures, fearing an attack by Bedouin, had taken a lot of the finest manuscripts to a cave known only to himself and his assistant. The attack came, both of them were killed, and the manuscripts were never found.[2] So do these still lie in such a cave? The frustrating feature is that many of those around Mar Saba have mouths so small that they are almost invisible from below, and can only be reached by skilled climbers. So if any such hoard is still buried in the region, it may keep its secret for some while yet.

Not even these possibilities end the list of books which, if re-discovered, might give us further authentic sayings of Jesus. Another such is Papias's five book *Expositions of the Sayings of the Lord*, extracts from which, as preserved by Eusebius, have been quoted earlier in this book. The very title of Papias's work seems to offer tremendous promise, allied to which we know it to have been written sometime before AD 130.

However, although this undoubtedly had some most valuable information on early gospels and their authors, we also know from Eusebius that Papias could be uncritical in what he collected. An extract from him quoted by Irenaeus, which actually includes a particularly long saying attributed to Jesus, is also self-evidently one of the least convincing of our entire collection:

> The days shall come wherein vines shall grow, each having ten thousand shoots and on one shoot ten thousand branches and on one branch ten thousand tendrils, and on every tendril ten thousand clusters, and in every cluster ten thousand grapes, and every grape when it is pressed shall yield five and twenty measures of wine. And when any of the saints shall take hold of one of the clusters, another will cry out: 'I am a better cluster, take me, through me bless thou the Lord'.
>
> Likewise also a grain of wheat shall bring forth ten thousand ears and every ear shall have ten thousand grains, and every grain shall yield five double pounds of white clean flour; and all other fruits and seeds and plants [shall yield] in the same proportion; and all animals shall use those foods which are got from the earth and shall be peaceable and in concord with one another, subject unto men with all obedience.[3]

As the New Testament scholar Joachim Jeremias remarked though, such language is not uncommon in late Jewish apocalyptic literature:

> Fantasy has run riot in this picture of the fertility which will follow when nature is renewed. It has surely nothing to do with Jesus.[4]

Finally, another most useful find in some yet-to-be discovered manuscript hoard could be the five books of 'Memoirs' against the Gnostics known to have been written by the second-century Jewish-born historian Hegesippus. As usual, most of our information on this early author comes from Eusebius, but if we possessed his complete text this might throw the new light we badly need on Jesus's earliest Jewish followers, and thereby perhaps give us a better understanding of some of the sayings that we do possess. That the possibility of finding a copy of Hegesippus is no pipe-dream is suggested by the fact that complete copies of his 'Memoirs' are said to have existed in some libraries even as late as the sixteenth and seventeenth centuries.[5]

Accordingly there is every reason to hope that our present stock of sayings of Jesus, canonical and non-canonical, may some day be quite dramatically increased. We might find ourselves gripped by some really convincing new sayings, challenged by striking fresh parables, or provided with totally new insights into some of the many still unknown incidents of Jesus's life. Anything of this kind would unquestionably be of enormous interest value.

But in the end we do not need it. The message of Jesus remains with us, as it has over the last two thousand years, in an unshatterable entirety that will ever demand more of us than we can live up to while we continue to cling to the world of all our material possessions and yet more material values.

For no one really needs any more abundance of Jesus's words, or any further test of them. Their proof and their permanence lies in their very absurdity and insubstantiality. Ostensibly it has to be an insane sort of faith that demands that the rich man sell all his possessions; that tells the poor and oppressed to be happy in their sufferings; that asks not revenge, but love for the most hardened terrorist; not persecution but forgiveness for the thief, the adulterer and the prostitute. Traced in the dust words of this kind seem so insubstantial that the slightest breeze ought to be able to blow them away. Yet these words have lasted, and will continue to last. Written into our hearts they are truly of the very stuff to move mountains, continents, even a whole planet.

Notes

Introduction

1 T.R. Glover, *The Jesus of History*, London, SCM, 1917, pp.4-5.

Chapter 1

1 The dating of the gospels has long been a matter of debate among New Testament scholars. According to the most widely held view, ably outlined in Werner Kümmel's *Introduction to the New Testament*, trans. A.J. Mattill, London, SCM Press, 1966, the four gospels were written between AD 70 and AD 100, that is, about and after the fall of Jerusalem in AD 70. But in 1976 this view was challenged by the late Dr John A.T. Robinson in his *Redating the New Testament*, London, SCM Press, 1976. Robinson argued for all gospels having been completed before AD 70, pointing out in particular how the gospel writers otherwise failed to capitalise on the apparent fulfilment of Jesus's prophecy relating to Jerusalem's fall.

2 Although Papias's *Exposition of the Sayings of the Lord* has been lost, the quotation from it derives from Eusebius of Caesarea's *History of the Church*, trans. G.A. Williamson, Harmondsworth, Penguin, 1965, p.152.

3 For the broad evidence of all this, see B.H. Streeter's still unsurpassed classic *The Four Gospels, A Study of Origins*, London, Macmillan, 1927.

4 One of the pioneer scholars in the study of the 'link' passages was the German pastor Karl Ludwig Schmidt – see my own *Jesus: the Evidence*, p.38, London, Weidenfeld & Nicholson, 1984. 'Form-Criticism school' – in German *Formgeschichte* – is the attempt to trace the provenance and assess the historicity of particular Biblical passages by a close analysis of their structural forms.

5 Clement of Alexandria *Stromateis*, 3.9.64 and 66: 3.13.92; and 3.6.45. For quotations see M.R. James, *The Apocryphal New Testament*, Oxford, Clarendon Press, corrected ed. 1953, pp.10-12.

6 Origen, 'Homily on Luke', quoted in M.R. James, *op.cit.*, p.10.

7 Jerome, *On Matthew* xii, 13.

8 Eusebius, trans. Williamson, *op.cit.*, p.137.

9 *Ibid*, pp.213-14.

10 For details of the Gelasian Decree, see M.R. James, *op.cit.*, pp.21-3.

Chapter 2

1 G.A. Wells, *The Jesus of the Early Christians*, London, Pemberton, 1971; *Did Jesus Exist?* New York, Prometheus, 1975; *The Historical Evidence for Jesus*, New York, Prometheus, 1982.

2 John Allegro, *The Sacred Mushroom and the Cross*, London, Hodder, 1970.

3 There is no certainty on the year of Jesus's death. It was clearly within the governorship of Pontius Pilate, whose term of administration is known to have been between AD 27 and 36. But John and the synoptic writers seem to differ over whether the actual day of Jesus's Crucifixion was 'Passover Preparation Day', thus preventing any certainty of calculations.

4 B. Metzger, 'Recently Published Greek Papyri of the New Testament', *Biblical Archaeologist*, 10, 2 May 1947, p.38.

5 See R. Steck, 'Professor Schmiedels Grundsäulen des Lebens Jesu und ihre amerikanische Bestreitung', *Protestantische Monatschefte*, xxv, 1921, pp.161-7.

6 T.R. Glover, *The Jesus of History*, London, SCM Press, 1917, pp.83-4.

7 Adolf Deissman, *Light from the Ancient East*, London, Hodder & Stoughton, 1927, p.33.

8 *Ibid*, p.187.

9 Geza Vermes, *Jesus the Jew*, London, Collins, 1973, p.52.

10 Don Cupitt and Peter Armstrong, *Who was Jesus?*, London, BBC, 1977, p.53.

Chapter 3

1 For an introduction to the Gnostics and their writings, see particularly Elaine Pagels, *The Gnostic Gospels*, London, Weidenfeld, 1980; also Tobias Churton, *The Gnostics*, London, Weidenfeld & Nicholson, 1988.

2 For a fuller background to the so-called 'Pericope Adulterae', see J.H. Bernard, *St John*, London, International Critical Commentary, 1928, pp.715-21.

3 Eusebius (quoting Papias), *History of the Church*, trans. G.A. Williamson, Harmondsworth, Penguin, 1965, p.153.

4 *Ibid.*, p.182.

5 Jerome, *Dialogue against Pelagius*, iii, 2. Translation modernised by the author, after M.R. James, *The Apocryphal New Testament*, Oxford, Clarendon Press, 1953, p.6.

6 *Ibid.*

7 Jerome, *On Ephesians*, v.4, modernised translation after M.R. James, *op.cit.*, p.3.

8 Eusebius, *Theophany*, 4, 12, modernised translation after M.R. James, pp.2-3.

9 Clement of Alexandria, *Stromateis*, 1.9.45 and 5.14.96.

10 Jerome, *Of Illustrious Men*, modernised translation after Robert M. Grant and David Noel Freedman, *The Secret Sayings of Jesus according to the Gospel of Thomas*, London, Collins, 1960, p.32.

11 Eusebius (quoting Hegesippus), trans. Williamson, *op.cit.*, pp.99 ff.

12 *Ibid* (quoting Clement), p.72.

13 Clement of Alexandria, *Stromateis*, 3, 64, 1 (3, 45, 3); 3, 66, 1-2; 3, 92, 2, after Grant and Freedman, *op.cit.*, pp.33-4.

14 Clement of Alexandria, *Stromateis*, 3, 63, 1-2.

Chapter 4

1 See H.B. Swete, *The Akhmim Fragment of the Apocryphal Gospel of St Peter*, London, Macmillan, 1893; also complete text of this as quoted in Grant and Freedman, *The Secret Sayings of Jesus According to the Gospel of Thomas*, London, Collins, 1960, p.36.

2 Eusebius (quoting Serapion), *History of the Church*, trans. G.A. Williamson, Harmondsworth, Penguin, 1965, p.252.

3 Translation modernised by the author, after B. Metzger, *Manuscripts of the Greek Bible, An Introduction to Palaeography*, Oxford University Press, 1981.

4 Translation by C.H. Dodd, from H.I. Bell, *Recent Discoveries of Biblical Papyri*, Oxford, Clarendon Press, 1937, p.19.

5 B.P. Grenfell, 'The Oldest Record of Christ. The First Complete Account of the "Sayings of Our Lord"', intro. by F.G. Kenyon, *McClure's*, 11, 1897, p.1030.

6 This and subsequent translations modernised after B.P. Grenfell and A.S. Hunt *The Oxyrhynchus Papyri*, vols 125; Grant and Freedman, *op.cit.*, pp.44-49; and M.R. James, *The Apocryphal New Testament*, Oxford, Clarendon Press, 1953, pp.25-8.

7 Clement of Alexandria, *Stromateis*, 1, 9, 45.

8 H.G. Evelyn White, *The Sayings of Jesus from Oxyrhynchus*, Cambridge, 1920.

Chapter 5

1 For detailed but sometimes conflicting accounts of the Nag Hammadi discovery, see J.M. Robinson (ed.), *The Nag Hammadi Library*, New York, Harper and Row, 3rd edition 1989, pp.22 ff.; Elaine Pagels, *The Gnostic Gospels*, London, Weidenfeld, 1980; also Churton, *op.cit.*, p.8 ff.

2 This and subsequent translations now derived from J.M. Robinson, *op.cit.*, pp.126-38.

3 J. Doresse, *Secret Books of the Egyptian Gnostics*, London, Hollis and Carter, 1959.

4 G. Quispel, 'The Gospel of Thomas and the New Testament', *Vigiliae Christianae*, xi, 1957, pp.189-207.

5 Eusebius, trans. Williamson, *op.cit.*, p.107.

6 There is an extensive literature on the Malabar Christians, and the date of the original Christian evangelisation of India. See the biblography for the entry 'Malabar Christians' in the *Oxford Dictionary of the Christian Church*, ed. Cross, London, Oxford University Press, 1957.

7 See A. Roberts and J. Donaldson, *The Ante-Nicene Fathers*, vol viii, Michigan, Eerdmans, 1951, p.538 ff.

8 M.R. James, *The Apocryphal New Testament*, Oxford, Clarendon Press, 1953, p.49, also Roberts and Donaldson, *op.cit.*, p.395 ff.

9 Cyril, *Catech.*, iv, 36.

10 *Ibid*, vi, 31.

11 This is not in surviving manuscripts of Josephus, but is mentioned both by Origen and Eusebius; see the latter in

the Williamson translation, *op.cit.*, p.102.

12 H.C. Puech, 'Un logion de Jésus sur bandelette funéraire', *Revue de l'histoire des religions*, cxlvii, 1955, pp.126-9.

13 Grant and Freedman, *The Secret Sayings of Jesus According to the Gospel of Thomas*, London, Collins, 1960, p.67.

Chapter 6

1 J.M.Robinson (ed.), *The Nag Hammadi Library*, New York, Harper & Row, 3rd edition, 1989.

2 *Ibid.*, pp.246-55.

3 *Ibid.*, pp.141-56.

4 Quoted, without information on source, in the introduction to J.M. Robinson, *op.cit.*, p.5.

Chapter 7

1 For a fuller, popular presentation of the material discussed in this chapter, see Morton Smith, *The Secret Gospel*, London, Gollancz, 1974; and for the complete scholarly apparatus the same author's *Clement of Alexandria and a Secret Gospel of Mark*, Harvard University Press, 1973.

2 The full text is included in the appendix of this book, on p.175.

3 Eusebius (quoting Papias) trans. Williamson, *op.cit.*, p.152.

4 *Ibid.*, p.89.

Chapter 8

1 Luther made the remark in his preface to the edition of the New Testament published by him in 1522. See Roland H. Bainton, *Here I Stand, A Life of Martin Luther*, Nashville, Mentor, 1955, p.259.

2 Eusebius, trans. Williamson, *op.cit.*, pp. 99-100.

3 Josephus, *Antiquities*, 20, 9, 1, as quoted in Eusebius, trans. Williamson, *op.cit.*, p.103.

4 *Ibid.*, p.101.

5 John A.T. Robinson, *Redating the New Testament*, London, SCM Press, 1976, p.118ff.

6 Quoted without information on source in Roderic Dunkerley, *Beyond the Gospels*, Harmondsworth, Penguin, 1957, p.13.

7 *Ibid.*

8 J.N. Sevenster, 'Do You Know Greek? How much Greek could the First Jewish Christians have known?', *Nov. Test.* Supple. 19, Leiden, 1968, 3-21.

9 Eusebius (quoting Hegesippus), trans. Williamson, *op.cit.*, p.125.

Chapter 9

1 That the name at least is credible is indicated by a first-century Roman tombstone of one Julius Abdes Pantera, an archer from Sidon, found at Bingerbrück in Germany. See my *Jesus: the Evidence*, pp.63, 64.

2 Joseph Klausner, *Jesus of Nazareth, His Life, Times and Teaching*, London, Allen and Unwin, 1928, p.35.

3 *Sanh.* 107 b; *Sota* 47b; *J.Hag.* II 2(p.74-7). Modernised translation after Klausner, *op.cit.*, p.25.

4 *Shab.* 115 a and b, modernised translation after Klausner, *op.cit.*, p.44.

5 *Ab. Zar.* 16b-17a; *T. Hulin*, II 24, modernised translation after Klausner, *op.cit.*, pp.37-8.

6 Joseph Klausner was a renowned Hebrew scholar who wrote for fellow Jews, not Christians.

7 J. Jeremias, *Unknown Sayings of Jesus*, p.11.

8 N.J. Dawood (trans.), *The Koran*, Harmondsworth, Penguin, 1956, p.34. For clarity I have substituted 'God' for Allah when using this translation.

9 *Ibid.*, pp.103-4.

10 *Ibid.*, p.387.

11 Quoted in R. Dunkerley, *Beyond the Gospels*, Harmondsworth, Penguin, 1957, p.146.

12 *Ibid.*

13 Described and commented on during the last century by Alexander Duff: *Life*, 1879; also C.F. Gordon-Cumming, *In the Himalayas*, 1884.

Chapter 10

1 J.B. Segal, *Edessa the Blessed City*, Oxford, Clarendon Press, 1970, pp.62–3.

2 Eusebius trans. Williamson, *op.cit.*, p.66.

3 *Ibid.*

4 See reference in Segal, *op.cit.*, p.20, n.3.

5 W. Cureton, *Ancient Syriac Documents Relative to the Earliest Establishment of Christianity in Edessa*, London, 1864.

6 G. Philips *The Doctrine of Addai the Apostle*, 1876.

7 The Syriac 'Acts of Thaddaeus', as translated in Segal, *op.cit.*, p.62.

8 This is because of a variety of anachronisms indicative of this later date.

9 For a full translation, see Segal, *op.cit.*, pp.24–5.

10 For an excellent discussion of the Abgar VIII coinage, see Stauffer, *Christ and the Caesars*, London, SCM Press, 1955.

11 This refers to the *Vita Alexius*, a story that enjoyed wide popularity during the early Middle Ages; see Segal, *op.cit.*, p.173.

12 John Wilkinson, *Egeria's Travels*, London, SPCK, 1972, pp.115-17.

13 See J. Daniélou, 'Christianity as a Jewish Sect' in A. Toynbee (ed.), *The Crucible of Christianity*, London, Thames and Hudson, 1969, p.277.

14 Segal, *op.cit.*, p.78

15 Translation from G. Philips, *op.cit.*, p.45.

Chapter 11

1 St John Chrysostom, *Hom de Statius XIV Ad. Pop. Ant.*.

2 J. Jeremias, *Unknown Sayings of Jesus*, London, SPCK, 1957.

3 Translation from Grant and Freedman, *op.cit.*, pp.49-50.

4 E. Schürer, *History of the Jewish People in the Time of Jesus Christ*, 5 vols, 1890-1.

5 See for example the comments in Grant and Freedman, *op.cit.*, p.50.

6 J. Jeremias, *op.cit.*, p.44.

7 See extract from Eusebius *Theophany*, quoted in M.R. James, *op.cit.*, p.3.

8 First Letter of Clement, quoted in Dunkerley, *op.cit.*, pp.79-80, translation modernised by the author.

9 Epistle of Polycarp to the Philippians, quoted Dunkerley, *op.cit.*, p.83.

10 Second Letter of Clement, quoted in Dunkerley, p.87, translation modernised by the author.

11 See A.L. Williams, 'The Date of the Epistle of Barnabas', *Journal of Theological Studies*, xxxiv, 1933, pp.337-46.

12 Translation after Dunkerley p.82.

13 *Ibid.*, p.92.

14 Modernised translation by the author, after M.R. James, *op.cit.*, pp.31-2.

15 Modernised translation by the author, after Dunkerley, *op.cit.*, pp.143-4.

Chapter 12

1 Robert Houston Smith, 'A Sarcophagus from Pella', *Archaeology*, 26, pp.250-7.

2 Morton Smith, *The Secret Gospel*, London, Gollancz, 1974, p.4.

3 Translation after Dunkerley, p.85.

4 J. Jeremias, *Unknown Sayings of Jesus*, London, SPCK, 1957, p.9.

5 See entry 'Hegesippus' in *Oxford Dictionary of the Christian Church*, (ed.) Cross, London, Oxford University Press, 1957, p.617.

Appendix

The Documents

FROM THE BOOK OF ACTS

There is more happiness in giving than receiving.

(Acts 20:35)

(i) SCRAPS FROM THE FATHERS

From the 'Gospel of the Hebrews':

Some reported sayings:

On the same day, seeing a man working on the Sabbath, he said to him, 'If you know what you are doing, you are a happy man! But if you do not know, you are accursed and a Lawbreaker'.

(from the *Codex Bezae*, at Luke 6:5)

He who seeks will not cease until he finds; when he finds he will be astonished; when he is astonished, he will reign; when he reigns, he will rest.

(Quoted Clement of Alexandria *Stromateis* 1.9.45, as quoted in M.R. James *The Apocryphal New Testament* p.2)

Even now my mother the Holy Spirit took me and carried me up to the great Mount Tabor.

(Quoted by Origen, commenting on John 2:12 and Jeremiah in homily 15.4, as quoted in M.R. James *The Apocryphal New Testament* p.2)

I choose for myself the best that my Father who is in heaven gives me.

(Eusebius, *Theophany* 4.2, as quoted in M.R. James, p.23)

> Never be glad, except when you look upon your brother with love.
>
> (Quoted by St Jerome, commenting on Ephesians 5:4 as quoted in M.R. James *The Apocryphal New Testament* p.3)

> For the prophets also, even after being anointed by the Holy Spirit, could be found to be sinful.
>
> (Jerome, *Dialogue against Pelagius* iii, 2 as quoted in M.R. James *The Apocryphal New Testament* p.6)

An account of Jesus's baptism:

> Behold the mother of the Lord and his brothers said to him, 'John is baptising for the remission of sins; let us go and be baptised by him'. But he said to them, 'What sin have I committed, that I should go and be baptised by him – unless perhaps this very statement that I have made is ignorance?'.
>
> (Jerome: *Dialogue against Pelagius* iii, 2)

The story of the woman taken in adultery: unreproduced as it is available in all modern Bibles at John 8:3–11; also page 34 of this book.

(Mentioned by Eusebius in *History of the Church* 3, 39.17)

A mysterious and unparalleled account of Jesus's post-Resurrection appearance to his brother James:

> But the Lord, when he had given the *sindon* to the high priest's servant, went to James and appeared to him. For James had sworn that he would not eat bread from that hour when he had drunk the Lord's cup until he saw him rising from those who sleep ... 'Bring,' says the Lord, 'a table and bread'. He took bread and blessed it and broke it and gave it to James the Righteous and said to him, 'My brother, eat your bread, for the Son of Man has risen from those who sleep'.
>
> (Jerome *De Viris Illustribus*, 2 as quoted in M.R. James *The Apocryphal New Testament*, p.3)

From the 'Gospel of the Egyptians':

> Salome said, 'How long will men die?'.
>
> The Lord replied, 'As long as you women have children'.

Salome replied, 'I did well, then, by not having children'.

The Lord said, 'Eat every plant, but do not eat the one which contains bitterness'.

Salome asked when what she was inquiring about would be known.

The Lord said, 'When you trample on the garment of shame, and when the two become one, and the male with the female neither male nor female'.

(Clement of Alexandria, *Stromateis* 3.64.1(3.45.3); 3.66.1–2; 3.92.2, trans. as in Grant and Freedman, *Secret Sayings*, p.33)

The Saviour himself said, 'I came to destroy the works of the female'.

(*Stromateis* 3.63.1–2 translation as above)

(ii) MANUSCRIPT FRAGMENTS

From an unknown gospel manuscript of circa AD 150:

Fragment 1: verso:

[And Jesus said] to the lawyers, '[?Punish] every criminal and law-breaker, and not me ...'. And turning to the people's leaders he spoke this saying, 'You study the scriptures, believing that in them you have eternal life; these same scriptures testify to me. Do not imagine that I am going to accuse you before my Father; you place your hopes on Moses, and Moses will be your accuser'. And when they said, 'We know well that God spoke to Moses, but as for you, we do not know where you come from,' Jesus answered and said to them, 'Now it is your lack of faith that is accused ...'.

Fragment 1: recto:

[?They urged] the crowds to [?take up] stones and stone him. And the leaders tried to lay hands on him to take him and[?hand him over] to the crowds; but they could not arrest him, because his time of betrayal had not yet come. And he slipped through the crowds. And a leper came up to him and said, 'Rabbi Jesus, through travelling with lepers and having meals with them at the inn, I too have become a leper. If you want to, you can cure me'. Jesus then said to him, 'Of course I want to! Be cured!'. And his leprosy was cured at once. [And Jesus said to him] 'Go [and show yourself] to the [priests]'.

Fragment 2: recto:

... coming up to him began to test him with a question, saying, 'Rabbi Jesus, we know you are from God, for the prophets testify to the things you do. Tell us, then: Is it permissible [?to pay] taxes to those who rule over us? [Should we pay them], or not?'. But Jesus, reading their thoughts, said to them indignantly, 'Why do you call me Rabbi, when you don't listen to what I tell you? It was of you that Isaiah so rightly prophesied when he said, "This people honours me only with lip-service, while their hearts are far from me. The worship they offer me is worthless, [the doctrines they teach are only human] regulations ..."'.

Fragment 2: verso:

shut up ... in ... place ... its weight unweighed? And when they were puzzled at his strange question Jesus, as he walked, stood still on the edge of the river Jordan, and stretching out his right hand he ... and sprinkled it on the ... And then ... water that had been sprinkled ... before them began to bear fruit ...

(Egerton Papyrus 2, portions of three leaves of a papyrus in the British Museum)

From papyrus fragment of gospel as found by Grenfell and Hunt in 1897, subsequently identified as the 'Gospel of Thomas':

recto:

... and then you will clearly see to cast the mote from your brother's eye.

Jesus said: 'If you do not fast from the world, you will not find the kingdom of God, and if you do not keep the Sabbath for the whole week, you will not see the Father'.

Jesus said, 'I stood in the midst of the world, and I appeared to them in flesh: and I found all men drunk, with no one of them thirsty. And my soul grieves for the sons of men, because their hearts are blind and they do not see ...'.

verso:

> [Jesus said] 'Wherever there are two [they are not without] God, and wherever there is one alone I say I am with him. Raise the stone, and there you will find me. Cleave the wood, and I am there'.
>
> Jesus said, 'No prophet is accepted in his own country, nor can a physician heal those who know him'.
>
> Jesus said, 'A city built on the top of a high mountain and fortified can neither fall, nor be hidden'.
>
> Jesus said, 'You hear with one ear what ...'.
>
> (Papyrus Oxyrhynchus I.1)

From further papyrus fragments, subsequently identified as from the 'Gospel of Thomas', as found at Oxyrhynchus in 1903:

> These are the [...] words which the living Jesus [...] spoke to [...] and to Thomas. And he said [whoever hears] these words shall not taste [death].
>
> [Jesus said] 'Let not him who seeks cease [until he] finds, and when he finds [he will be astonished]; when he is astonished, he will reign; [when he reigns] he will rest'.
>
> Jesus said [...] who draw us [...] the kingdom in heaven [...] the birds of the heaven [...] what under the earth [...] the fishes of the sea [...] you and the kingdom [...] is within you [...] know you will find it [...] to know yourselves [...] you are of the Father who [...] you know yourselves in [...] and you are the [...].
>
> [...] a man will not hesitate to ask [...] about the place of [...] you, that many will be [...] and the last, first, and [...] will ...
>
> Jesus said: '[everything not] before your sight and [what is hidden] from you will be revealed [to you. Nothing] hidden will not [become] manifest and buried which will not be [raised]'.
>
> They ask him [his disciples and] say: 'How shall we fast [and how] shall be [...] and how [...] and what shall we observe [...]' Jesus said '[...] will be. Do not do [...] of truth [...] hidden [...] blessed is [...]'
>
> (Papyrus Oxyrhynchus IV, 654)
>
> ... from morning until evening [nor] from evening [until] morning nor [for] your [food] what you will eat [nor] for [your] rai[ment]

what you will wear. You are much better than the [li]lies, which neither card nor spin [...] having one gar[ment] why do you [...] in [...]

Who would add to your statute? He himself will give you your garment. They say to him, his disciples, When will you be visible to us and when shall we see you? he says, When you are stripped and are not ashamed [...]

They [took the key] of [knowledge] and [hid] it; they did not [enter [in, nor to those] entering [did they [open ... but you] be [come pru]dent a[s] serpents and sincere [as doves]...

(Papyrus Oxyrhynchus IV, 655,
translations based on Grant and Freedman,
Secret Sayings pp.44–9)

From a miniaturised manuscript, c.AD 400, of an unknown gospel, found at Oxyrhynchus in 1905:

First, before he does wrong [?], he uses every artifice. But be careful, in case you also suffer in the same way as them. For not only in life [?] do wrong-doers receive human chastisement, they must also suffer punishment and great torment.

... and he took them with him into the very place of purity and walked into the Temple. And a certain Pharisee, a chief priest, Levi by name, came to meet them and said to the Saviour,

'Who permitted you to walk upon this place of purity and look upon these holy vessels, when you have not first washed and your disciples have not washed their feet? But you have walked on this sacred spot in a state of defilement, this clean place, on which no one can walk unless he has washed and has changed his clothes, nor can he venture to look upon these holy vessels'.

The Saviour stopped with his disciples and answered,

'Since you are in the Temple, are you clean?'.

He says to him,

'I am clean; for I have washed in the pool of David and I went down to it by one ladder and up by another, and I have put on clean white clothing, and then I came and looked at these holy vessels'.

The Saviour answered and said to him,

'Woe to the blind who do not see! You have washed in these waters poured forth, in which dogs and swine lie night and day; and you have washed and scoured your outside skin, which harlots and flute girls anoint and wash and scour and beautify to arouse men's lust, though inwardly it is full of scorpions, and all unrighteousness. But I and my [disciples], whom you call unwashed, we have bathed in living waters [...] which have come from [...] But woe to the ...'

(Papyrus Oxyrhynchus V,840)

Fragment of sixth-century Coptic papyrus, apparently from an unidentified gospel, as found with the apocryphal 'Acts of Paul':

recto:

... the doings ...

... they were awestruck and deeply puzzled. He asked them 'Why are you so astonished that I can raise the dead, or help the lame to walk, or cure lepers, or heal the sick? Or that I have helped the paralysed and the possessed? Or that I have broken a few loaves and fed whole crowds? Or that I have walked on the sea? Or that I have controlled tempests? If you really believe this and are convinced, then you are very worthy: for truly, if you say to this mountain, throw yourself into the sea, without having any doubt in your mind, then it will happen ...'. One of those who was convinced was called Simon. He said, 'Lord, your doings are truly wonderful, for we have never before seen or heard ...'.

verso:

... ever anyone raised the dead, except you. The Lord told him: 'You will pray for those deeds which I shall do ... But the others I will carry out immediately. These I perform as a temporary means of salvation, wherever they occur, to aid faith in Him who sent me'. Simon said to him, 'Lord, permit me to speak'. He replied: 'Speak, Peter,' for from that time on he addressed them each by name. He said: 'What work can be greater than these ... except raising the dead, and feeding such huge crowds?'. The Lord said to him: 'There are some things even greater than this, and happy are those who have wholeheartedly believed'. But Philip raised his voice angrily, saying, 'What sort of teaching is this?'. But he told him: 'You ...'.

(Coptic MS at Heidelberg)

(iii) THE NAG HAMMADI COLLECTION

Some Sayings indicative of the arcane and unconvincing nature of much of the Gnostic material:

From the *Second Treatise of the Great Seth* (Nag Hammadi Codex 7, book 2):

> For my death, which they think happened, happened to them in their error and blindness, since they nailed their man unto their death.
>
> It was another upon whom they placed the crown of thorns. But I was rejoicing in the height over all the wealth of the archons and the offspring of their error, of their empty glory. And I was laughing at their ignorance.

From the Dialogue of the Saviour (Nag Hammadi Codex 3, book 5):

> [Matthew] said, 'Lord, I want [to see] that place of life [...] where there is no wickedness, [but rather] there is pure [light]'.
>
> The Lord [said], 'Brother [Matthew], you will not be able to see it [as long as you are] carrying flesh around'.
>
> ('Dialogue' 27, 28)
>
> If [one] does not [understand how] fire came into existence, he will burn in it, because he does not know the root of it. If one does not first understand water, he knows nothing. For what use is there for him to be baptised in it? If one does not understand how blowing wind came into existence, he will blow away with it. If one does not understand how the body, which he bears, came into existence, he will [perish] with it ...
>
> ('Dialogue' 35)
>
> [You have] asked me about a saying [...] which eye has not seen, [nor] have I heard it except from you. But I say to you that when what invigorates a man is removed, he will be called 'dead'. And when what is alive leaves what is dead, what is alive will be called upon.
>
> ('Dialogue' 57)
>
> Whatever is born of truth does not die. Whatever is born of woman dies.
>
> ('Dialogue' 59)

> The Lord said, 'Pray in the place where there is no woman'.
>
> ('Dialogue' 91)

From the 'Gospel of Philip' (Nag Hammadi Codex 2, book 3):

> The Lord said to the disciples '[...] from every house. Bring into the house of my father. But do not take (anything) in the house of the father nor carry it off'.
>
> ('Philip' 55:37 to 56:3)

> He said on that day in the thanksgiving, 'You who have joined the perfect light with the holy spirit, unite the angels with us also, as being the images'.
>
> ('Philip' 58:10–14)

> ... a disciple asked the Lord one day for something of this world. He said to him, 'Ask your mother, and she will give you of the things which are another's'.
>
> ('Philip' 59:25–27)

> The Lord went into the dye works of Levi. He took seventy-two different colours and threw them into the vat. He took them out all white. And he said, 'Even so has the son of man come as a dyer'.
>
> ('Philip' 63:29,30)

> [The Lord loved] Mary Magdalen ... more than [all] the disciples [and used to] kiss her [often] on her [...] The rest of [the disciples ...] They said to him, 'Why do you love her more than all of us?'. The Saviour answered and said to them, 'Why do I not love you like her? When a blind man and one who sees are both together in darkness, they are no different from one another. When the light comes, then he who sees will see the light, and he who is blind will remain in darkness'.
>
> ('Philip' 64:2–9)

> The Lord said, 'Blessed is he who is before he came into being. For he who is, has been and shall be'.
>
> ('Philip' 64:10–12)

> [...] he said, 'I came to make [the things below] like the things [above, and the things] outside like those [inside. I came to unite] them in the place'.
>
> ('Philip' 67:30–35)

> The Lord said it well: 'Some have entered the kingdom of heaven

laughing, and they have come out [...] because [...] a Christian, [...]'.

('Philip' 74:25–28)

From the *'Gospel of Thomas'* (Nag Hammadi Codex 2, book 2):

These are the secret sayings which the living Jesus spoke and which Dydmos Judas Thomas wrote down.

1. And he said, 'Whoever finds the interpretation of these sayings will not experience death'.

2. Jesus said, 'Let him who seeks continue seeking until he finds. When he finds he will become troubled. When he becomes troubled, he will be astonished, and he will rule over all'.

3. Jesus said, 'If those who lead you say to you, "See, the Kingdom is in the sky", then the birds of the sky will precede you. If they say to you, "It is in the sea", then the fish will precede you. Rather, the Kingdom is inside of you, and it is outside of you. When you come to know yourselves, then you will become known, and you will realise that it is you who are the sons of the living Father. But if you will not know yourselves, you dwell in poverty and it is you who are that poverty'.

4. Jesus said, 'The man old in days will not hesitate to ask a small child seven days old about the place of life, and he will live. For many who are first will become last, and they will become one and the same'.

5. Jesus said, 'Recognise what is in your sight, and that which is hidden from you will become plain to you. For there is nothing hidden which will not become manifest'.

6. His disciples questioned him and said to him, 'Do you want us to fast? How shall we pray? Shall we give alms? What diet shall we observe?'.

Jesus said, 'Do not tell lies, and do not do what you hate, for all things are plain in the sight of Heaven. For nothing hidden will not become manifest, and nothing covered will remain without being uncovered'.

7. Jesus said, 'Blessed is the lion which becomes man when consumed by man; and cursed is the man whom the lion consumes, and the lion becomes man'.

8. And he said, 'The man is like a wise fisherman who cast his net into the sea and drew it up from the sea full of small fish. Among them the wise fisherman found a fine large fish. He threw all the small fish back into the sea and chose the large fish without difficulty. Whoever has ears to hear, let him hear'.

9. Jesus said, 'Now the sower went out, took a handful [of seeds], and scattered them. Some fell on the road; the birds came and gathered them up. Others fell on rock, did not take root in the soil, and did not produce ears. And others fell on thorns; they choked the seed(s) and worms ate them. And others fell on the good soil and produced good fruit: it bore sixty per measure and a hundred and twenty per measure'.

10. Jesus said, 'I have cast fire upon the world, and see, I am guarding it until it blazes'.

11. Jesus said, 'This heaven will pass away, and the one above it will pass away. The dead are not alive, and the living will not die. In the days when you consumed what is dead, you made it what is alive. When you come to dwell in the light, what will you do? On the day when you were one you became two. But when you become two, what will you do?'.

12. The disciples said to Jesus, 'We know that you will depart from us. Who is to become our leader?'. Jesus said to them, 'Wherever you are, you are to go to James the Righteous, for whose sake heaven and earth came into being'.

13. Jesus said to his disciples, 'Compare me to someone and tell me whom I am like'.

Simon Peter said to him, 'You are like a righteous angel'.

Matthew said to him, 'You are like a wise philosopher'.

Thomas said to him, 'Master, my mouth is wholly incapable of saying whom you are like'.

Jesus said, 'I am not your master. Because you have drunk, you have become intoxicated from the bubbling spring which I have measured out'.

And he took him and withdrew and told him three things. When Thomas returned to his companions, they asked him, 'What did Jesus say to you?'. Thomas said to them, 'If I tell you one of the things which he told me, you will pick up stones and throw them at me; a fire will come out of the stones and burn you up'.

14. Jesus said to them, 'If you fast, you will give rise to sins for yourselves; and if you pray, you will be condemned; and if you give alms, you will do harm to your spirits. When you go into any land and walk about in the districts, if they receive you, eat what they will set before you, and heal the sick among them. For what goes into your mouth will not defile you, but that which issues from your mouth – it is that which will defile you'.

15. Jesus said, 'When you see one who was not born of woman, prostrate yourselves on your faces and worship him. That one is your Father'.

16. Jesus said, 'Men think, perhaps, that it is peace which I have come to cast upon the world. They do not know that it is dissension which I have come to cast upon the earth: fire, sword, and war. For there will be five in a house: three will be against two, and two against three, the father against the son, and the son against the father. And they will stand solitary'.

17. Jesus said, 'I shall give you what no eye has seen and what no ear has heard and what no hand has touched and what has never occurred to the human mind'.

18. The disciples said to Jesus, 'Tell us how our end will be'.

Jesus said, 'Have you discovered, then, the beginning, that you look for the end? For where the beginning is, there will the end be. Blessed is he who will take his place in the beginning: he will know the end and will not experience death'.

19. Jesus said, 'Blessed is he who came into being before he came into being. If you become my disciples and listen to my words, these stones will minister to you. For there are five trees for you in Paradise which remain undisturbed summer and winter and whose leaves do not fall. Whoever becomes acquainted with them will not experience death'.

20. The disciples said to Jesus, 'Tell us what the Kingdom of Heaven is like'.

He said to them, 'It is like a mustard seed, the smallest of all seeds. But when it falls on tilled soil, it produces a great plant and becomes a shelter for birds of the sky'.

21. Mary said to Jesus, 'Whom are your disciples like?'.

He said, 'They are like children who have settled in a field which is not theirs. When the owners of the field come, they will say, "Let us have back our field". They [will] undress in their presence in order to let them have back their field and to give it back to them. Therefore I say to you, if the owner of the house knows that the thief is coming, he will begin his vigil before he comes and will not let him dig through into his house of his domain to carry away his goods. You, then, be on your guard against the world. Arm yourselves with great strength lest the robbers find a way to come to you, for the difficulty which you expect will [surely] materialise. Let there be among you a man of understanding. When the grain ripened, he came quickly with his sickle in his hand and reaped it. Whoever has ears to hear, let him hear'.

22. Jesus saw infants being suckled. He said to his disciples, 'These infants being suckled are like those who enter the Kingdom?'.

They said to him, 'Shall we then, as children, enter the Kingdom'.

Jesus said to them, 'When you make the two one, and when you make the inside like the outside and the outside like the inside, and the above like the below, and when you make the male and the female one and the same, so that male not be male nor the female female, and when you fashion eyes in the place of an eye, and a hand in place of a hand, and a foot in place of a foot, and a likeness in place of a likeness; then you will enter [the Kingdom]'.

23. Jesus said, 'I shall choose you, one out of a thousand, and two out of ten thousand, and they shall stand as a single one'.

24. His disciples said to him, 'Show us the place where you are, since it is necessary for us to seek it'.

He said to them, 'Whoever has ears, let him hear. There is light within a man of light, and he [or : it] lights up the whole world. If he [or : it] does not shine, he [or : it] is darkness'.

25. Jesus said, 'Love your brother like your soul, guard him like the pupil of your eye'.

26. Jesus said, 'You see the mote in your brother's eye, but you do not see the beam in your own eye. When you cast the beam out

of your own eye, then you will see clearly to cast the mote from your brother's eye'.

27. [Jesus said,] 'If you do not fast as regards the world, you will not find the Kingdom. If you do not observe the Sabbath as a Sabbath, you will not see the Father'.

28. Jesus said, 'I took my place in the midst of the world, and I appeared to them in flesh. I found all of them intoxicated; I found none of them thirsty. And my soul became afflicted for the sons of men, because they are blind in their hearts and do not have sight; for empty they came into the world, and empty too they seek to leave the world. But for the moment they are intoxicated. When they shake off their wine, then they will repent'.

29. Jesus said, 'If the flesh came into being because of spirit, it is a wonder. But if spirit came into being because of the body, it is a wonder of wonders. Indeed, I am amazed at how great this wealth has made its home in this poverty'.

30. Jesus said, 'Where there are three gods, they are gods. Where there are two or one, I am with him'.

31. Jesus said, 'No prophet is accepted in his own village; no physician heals those who know him'.

32. Jesus said, 'A city being built on a high mountain and fortified cannot fall, nor can it be hidden'.

33. Jesus said, 'Preach from your housetops that which you will hear in your ear. For no one lights a lamp and puts it under a bushel, nor does he put it in a hidden place, but rather he sets it on a lampstand so that everyone who enters and leaves will see its light'.

34. Jesus said, 'If a blind man leads a blind man, they will both fall into a pit'.

35. Jesus said, 'It is not possible for anyone to enter the house of a strong man and take it by force unless he binds his hands; then he will [be able to] ransack his house'.

36. Jesus said, 'Do not be concerned from morning until evening and from evening until morning about what you will wear'.

37. His disciples said, 'When will you become revealed to us and when shall we see you?'.

Jesus said, 'When you disrobe without being ashamed and take up your garments and place them under your feet like little children and tread on them, then [will you see] the Son of the Living One and you will not be afraid'.

38. Jesus said, 'Many times have you desired to hear these words which I am saying to you, and you have no one else to hear them from. There will be days when you will look for me and will not find me'.

39. Jesus said, 'The Pharisees and the scribes have taken the keys of Knowledge and hidden them. They themselves have not entered, nor have they allowed to enter those who wish to. You, however, be as wise as serpents and as innocent as doves'.

40. Jesus said, 'A grapevine has been planted outside of the Father, but being unsound, it will be pulled up by its roots and destroyed'.

41. Jesus said, 'Whoever has something in his hand will receive more, and whoever has nothing will be deprived of even the little he has'.

42. Jesus said, 'Become passers-by'.

43. His disciples said to him, 'Who are you, that you should say these things to us?'.

[Jesus said to them,] 'You do not realise who I am from what I say to you, but you have become like the Jews, for they (either) love the tree and hate its fruit (or) love the fruit and hate the tree'.

44. Jesus said, 'Whoever blasphemes against the Father will be forgiven, and whoever blasphemes against the Son will be forgiven, but whoever blasphemes against the Holy Spirit will not be forgiven either on earth or in heaven'.

45. Jesus said, 'Grapes are not harvested from thorns, nor are figs gathered from thistles, for they do not produce fruit. A good man brings forth good things from his storehouse; an evil man brings forth evil things from his evil storehouse, which is in his heart, and says evil things. For out of the abundance of the heart he brings forth evil things'.

46. Jesus said, 'Among those born of women, from Adam until John the Baptist, there is no one so superior to John the Baptist that

his eyes should not be lowered (before him). Yet I have said, whichever one of you comes to be a child will be acquainted with his Kingdom and will become superior to John'.

47. Jesus said, 'It is impossible for a man to mount two horses or to stretch two bows. And it is impossible for a servant to serve two masters; otherwise, he will honour the one and treat the other contemptuously. No man drinks old wine and immediately desires to drink new wine. And new wine is not put into old wineskins, lest they burst; nor is old wine put into a new wineskin, lest it spoil it. An old patch is not sown onto a new garment, because a tear would result'.

48. Jesus said, 'If two make peace with each other in this one house, they will say to the mountain, "Move away", and it will move away'.

49. Jesus said, 'Blessed are the solitary and elect, for you will find the Kingdom. For you are from it and to it you will return'.

50. Jesus said, 'If they say to you, "Where did you come from?" say to them, "We came from the light, the place where the light came into being on its own accord and established [itself] and became manifest through their image". If they say to you "Is it you?" say, "We are its children, and we are the elect of the Living Father". If they ask you, "What is the sign of your Father in you?" say to them, "It is movement and repose"'.

51. His disciples said to him, 'When will the repose of the dead come about, and when will the new world come?'.

He said to them, 'What you look forward to has already come, but you do not recognise it'.

52. His disciples said to him, 'Twenty-four prophets spoke in Israel, and all of them spoke in you'.

He said to them, 'You have omitted the one living in your presence and have spoken (only) of the dead'.

53. His disciples said to him, 'Is circumcision beneficial or not?'.

He said to them, 'If it were beneficial, their father would beget them already circumcised from their mother. Rather, the true circumcision in spirit has become completely profitable'.

54. Jesus said, 'Blessed are the poor, for yours is the Kingdom of

Heaven'.

55. Jesus said, 'Whoever does not hate his father and his mother cannot become a disciple to me. And whoever does not hate his brothers and sisters and take up his cross in my way will not be worthy of me'.

56. Jesus said, 'Whoever has come to understand the world has found (only) a corpse, and whoever has found a corpse is superior to the world'.

57. Jesus said, 'The Kingdom of the Father is like a man who had [good] seed. His enemy came by night and sowed weeds among the good seed. The man did not allow them to pull up the weeds; he said to them, "I am afraid that you will go intending to pull up the weeds and pull up the wheat along with them". For on the day of the harvest the weeds will be plainly visible, and they will be pulled up and burned'.

58. Jesus said, 'Blessed is the man who has suffered and found life'.

59. Jesus said, 'Take heed of the Living One while you are alive, lest you die and seek to see him and be unable to do so'.

60. [They saw] a Samaritan carrying a lamb on his way to Judea. He said to his disciples, '[Why does] that man [carry] the lamb around?'.

They said to him, 'So that he may kill it and eat it'.

He said to them, 'While it is alive, he will not eat it, but only when he has killed it and it has become a corpse'.

They said to him, 'He cannot do so otherwise'.

He said to them, 'You too, look for a place for yourselves within Repose, lest you become a corpse and be eaten'.

61. Jesus said, 'Two will rest on a bed: the one will die, and the other will live'.

Salome said, 'Who are you, man, that you, as though from the One, (or:[whose son]), that you have come up on my couch and eaten from my table?'.

Jesus said to her, 'I am He who exists from the Undivided. I was given some of the things of my Father'.

[Salome said,] 'I am your disciple'.

[Jesus said to her] 'Therefore I say, if he is [undivided], he will be filled with light, but if he is divided, he will be filled with darkness'.

62. Jesus said, 'It is to those [who are worthy of my] mysteries that I tell my mysteries. Do not let your left hand know what your right hand is doing'.

63. Jesus said, 'There was a rich man who had much money. He said, 'I shall put my money to use so that I may sow, reap, plant, and fill my storehouse with produce, with the result that I shall lack nothing.' Such were his intentions, but that same night he died. Let him who has ears hear'.

64. Jesus said, 'A man had received visitors. And when he had prepared the dinner, he sent his servants to invite the guests. He went to the first one and said to him, "My master invites you". He said, "I have claims against some merchants. They are coming to me this evening. I must go and give them my orders. I ask to be excused from the dinner.". He went to another and said to him, "My master has invited you". He said to him, "I have just bought a house and am required for the day. I shall not have any spare time". He went to another and said to him, "My master invites you". He said to him, "My friend is going to get married, and I am to prepare the banquet. I shall not be able to come. I ask to be excused from the dinner". He went to another and said to him, "My master invites you". He said to him, "I have just bought a farm, and I am on my way to collect the rent, I shall not be able to come, I ask to be excused". The servant returned and said to his master, "Those whom you invited to the dinner have asked to be excused". The master said to his servant, "Go outside to the streets and bring back those you happen to meet, so that they may dine". Businessmen and merchants will not enter the places of my Father'.

65. He said, 'There was a good man who owned a vineyard. He leased it to tenant farmers so that they might work it and he might collect the produce from them. He sent his servant so that the tenants might give him the produce of the vineyard. They seized his servant and beat him, all but killing him. The servant went back and told his master. The master said, "Perhaps [they] did not recognise [him]". He sent another servant. The tenants beat this

one as well. Then the owner sent his son and said, "Perhaps they will show respect to my son". Because the tenants knew that it was he who was the heir to the vineyard, they seized him and killed him. Let him who has ears hear'.

66. Jesus said, 'Show me the stone which the builders have rejected. That one is the cornerstone'.

67. Jesus said, 'Whoever believes that the All itself is deficient is [himself] completely deficient'.

68. Jesus said, 'Blessed are you when you are hated and persecuted. Wherever you have been persecuted they will find no place'.

69. Jesus said, 'Blessed are they who have been persecuted within themselves. It is they who have truly come to know the Father. Blessed are the hungry, for the belly of him who desires will be filled'.

70. Jesus said, 'That which you have will save you if you bring it forth from yourselves. That which you do not have within you will kill you if you do not have it within you'.

71. Jesus said, 'I shall destroy [this] house and no one will be able to rebuild it'.

72. [A man said] to him, 'Tell my brothers to divide my father's possessions with me'.

He said to him, 'O man, who has made me a divider?'. He turned to his disciples and said to them, 'I am not a divider, am I?'.

73. Jesus said, 'The harvest is great but the labourers are few. Beseech the Lord, therefore, to send out labourers to the harvest'.

74. He said, 'O Lord, there are many around the drinking trough, but there is nothing in the cistern'.

75. Jesus said, 'Many are standing at the door, but it is the solitary who will enter the bridal chamber'.

76. Jesus said, 'The Kingdom of the Father is like a merchant who had a consignment of merchandise and who discovered a pearl. That merchant was shrewd. He sold the merchandise and bought the pearl alone for himself. You too, seek his unfailing and enduring treasure where no moth comes near to devour and no worm destroys'.

77. Jesus said, 'It is I who am the light which is above them all. It is I who am the All. From me did the All come forth, and unto me did the All extend. Split a piece of wood, and I am there. Lift up the stone and you will find me there'.

78. Jesus said, 'Why have you come out into the desert? To see a reed shaken by the wind? And to see a man clothed in fine garments like your kings and your great men? Upon them are the [fine] garments, and they are unable to discern the truth'.

79. A woman from the crowd said unto him, 'Blessed are the womb which bore you and the breasts which nourished you'.

He said to her, 'Blessed are those who have heard the word of the Father and have kept it. For there will be days when you will say, "Blessed are the womb which has not conceived and the breasts which have not given milk"'.

80. Jesus said, 'He who has recognised the world has found the body, but he who has found the body is superior to the world'.

81. Jesus said, 'Let him who has grown rich be king, and let him who possesses power renounce it'.

82. Jesus said, 'He who is near me is near the fire, and he who is far from me is far from the Kingdom'.

83. Jesus said, 'The images are manifest to man, but the light in them remains concealed in the image of the light of the Father. He will become manifest, but his image will remain concealed by his light'.

84. Jesus said, 'When you see your likeness, you rejoice. But when you see your images which came into being before you, and which neither die nor become manifest, how much you will have to bear!'.

85. Jesus said, 'Adam came into being from a great power and a great wealth, but he did not become worthy of you. For had he been worthy, [he would] not [have experienced] death'.

86. Jesus said, '[The foxes have their holes] and the birds have [their] nests, but the Son of Man has no place to lay his head and rest'.

87. Jesus said, 'Wretched is the body that is dependent upon a

body, and wretched is the soul that is dependent on these two'.

88. Jesus said, 'The angels and the prophets will come to you and give to you those things you (already) have. And you too, give them those things which you have, and say to yourselves, "When will they come and take what is theirs?"'.

89. Jesus said, 'Why do you wash the outside of the cup? Do you not realise that he who made the inside is the same one who made the outside?'.

90. Jesus said, 'Come unto me, for my yoke is easy and my lordship is mild, and you will find repose for yourselves'.

91. They said to him, 'Tell us who you are so that we may believe in you'.

He said to them, 'You read the face of the sky and of the earth, but you have not recognised the one who [or: that which] is before you, and you do not know how to read this moment'.

92. Jesus said, 'Seek and you will find. Yet, what you asked me about in former times and which I did not tell you then, now I do desire to tell, but you do not enquire after it'.

93. [Jesus said,] 'Do not give what is holy to dogs, lest they throw them on the dung heap. Do not throw the pearls to swine, lest they grind it [to bits]'.

94. Jesus said, 'He who seeks will find, and [he who knocks] will be let in'.

95. [Jesus said], 'If you have money, do not lend it at interest, but give [it] to one from whom you will not get it back'.

96. Jesus [said], 'The Kingdom of the Father is like a certain woman. She took a little leaven, [concealed] it in some dough, and made it into large loaves. Let him who has ears hear'.

97. Jesus said, 'The Kingdom of the [Father] is like a certain woman who was carrying a jar full of meal. While she was walking [on] a road, still some distance from home, the handle of the jar broke and the meal emptied out behind her on the road. She did not realise it; she had noticed no accident. When she reached her house, she set the jar down and found it empty'.

98. Jesus said, 'The Kingdom of the Father is like a certain man

who wanted to kill a powerful man. In his own house he drew his sword and stuck it into the wall in order to find out whether his hand could carry through. Then he slew the powerful man'.

99. The disciples said to him, 'Your brothers and your mother are standing outside'.

He said to them, 'Those here who do the will of My Father are my brothers and my mother. It is they who will enter the Kingdom of My Father'.

100. They showed Jesus a gold coin and said to him, 'Caesar's men demand taxes from us'.

He said to them, 'Give Caesar what belongs to Caesar, give God what belongs to God, and give me what is mine'.

101. [Jesus said,] 'Whoever does not hate his father and his mother as I do cannot become a disciple to me. And whoever does [not] love his father and his mother as I do cannot become a [disciple] to me. For my mother [gave me falsehood], but [my] true [mother] gave me life'.

102. Jesus said, 'Woe to the Pharisees, for they are like a dog sleeping in the manger of oxen, for neither does he eat nor does he let the oxen eat'.

103. Jesus said, 'Fortunate is the man who knows where the brigands will enter, so that he may get up, muster his domain, and arm himself before they invade'.

104. They said [to Jesus], 'Come, let us pray today and let us fast'.

Jesus said, 'What is the sin that I have committed, or wherein have I been defeated? But when the bridegroom leaves the bridal chamber, then let them fast and pray'.

105. Jesus said, 'He who knows the father and mother will be called the son of a harlot'.

106. Jesus said, 'When you make the two one, you will become the sons of man, and when you say, "Mountain, move away", it will move away'.

107. Jesus said, 'The kingdom is like a shepherd who had a hundred sheep. One of them, the largest, went astray. He left the ninety-nine and looked for that one until he found it. When he had

gone to such trouble, he said to the sheep, "I care for you more than the ninety-nine"'.

108. Jesus said, 'He who will drink from my mouth will become like me. I myself shall become he, and the things that are hidden will be revealed to him'.

109. Jesus said, 'The Kingdom is like a man who had a [hidden] treasure in his field without knowing it. And [after] he died, he left it to his son. The son did not know [about the treasure]. He inherited the field and sold [it]. And the one who bought it went ploughing and found the treasure. He began to lend money at interest to whomever he wished'.

110. Jesus said, 'Whoever finds the world and becomes rich, let him renounce the world'.

111. Jesus said, 'The heavens and the earth will be rolled up in your presence. And the one who lives from the Living One will not see death'. Does not Jesus say, 'Whoever finds himself is superior to the world?'.

112. Jesus said, 'Woe to the flesh that depends on the soul; woe to the soul that depends on the flesh'.

113. His disciples said to him, 'When will the Kingdom come?'.

[Jesus said,] 'It will not come by waiting for it. It will not be a matter of saying "Here it is" or "There it is". Rather, the Kingdom of the Father is spread out upon the earth, and men do not see it'.

114. Simon Peter said to them, 'Let Mary leave us, for women are not worthy of Life'.

Jesus said, 'I myself shall lead her in order to make her male, so that she too may become a living spirit resembling you males. For every woman who will make herself male will enter the Kingdom of Heaven'.

(Translation: Thomas O. Lambdin, from J.M. Robinson, *The Nag Hammadi Library*, New York, Harper & Row, 3rd revised edition, 1989)

(iv) THE 'SECRET GOSPEL'

From a purported letter of Clement of Alexandria, copied into the back of a seventeenth-century printed edition of the letters of St Ignatius of Antioch, as kept in the library of Mar Saba:

> From the letters of the most holy Clement, author of the *Stromateis*. To Theodore:
>
> You did well in silencing the unspeakable teachings of the Carpocratians. For these are the 'wandering stars' referred to in the prophecy ...
>
> Now of the [things] they keep saying about the divinely inspired Gospel according to Mark, some are altogether falsifications, and others, even if they do contain some true [elements], nevertheless are not reported truly. For the true [things], being mixed with inventions, so that, as the saying [goes], even the salt loses its savour.
>
> [As for] Mark, then, during Peter's stay in Rome he wrote [an account of] the Lord's doings, not, however, declaring all [of them], nor yet hinting at the secret [ones], but selecting those he thought most useful for increasing the faith of those who were being instructed. But when Peter died as a martyr, Mark came over to Alexandria, bringing his own notes and those of Peter, from which he transferred to his former book the things suitable to whatever makes for progress towards knowledge [γνωσισ]. [Thus] he composed a more spiritual gospel for the use of those who were being perfected ... and dying he left his composition to the church in Alexandria, where it even yet is most carefully guarded ...
>
> But ... Carpocrates ... so enslaved a certain presbyter of the church in Alexandria that he got from him a copy of the secret Gospel, which he both interpreted according to his blasphemous and carnal doctrine and, moreover, polluted, mixing with the spotless and holy words utterly shameless lies. From this mixture is drawn off the teaching of the Carpocratians.
>
> To them, therefore ... one must never give way, nor ... should one concede that the secret Gospel is by Mark ... [But] to you ... I shall not hesitate to answer the [questions] you have asked, refuting the falsification by the very words of the Gospel. For example, after

'And they were in the road going up to Jerusalem,' and what follows, until 'After three days he shall arise,' [the secret Gospel] brings the following [material] word for word:

> 'And they came to Bethany, and a certain woman, whose brother had died, was there. And coming, she prostrated herself before Jesus and says to him, "Son of David, have mercy on me". But the disciples rebuked her. And Jesus, being angered, went off with her into the garden where the tomb was, and straightway a great cry was heard from the tomb. And going near, Jesus rolled away the stone from the door of the tomb. And straightway, going in where the youth was, he stretched forth his hand and raised him, seizing his hand. But the youth, looking upon him, loved him and began to beseech him that he might be with him. And going out of the tomb they came into the house of the youth, for he was rich. And after six days Jesus told him what to do and in the evening the youth comes to him, wearing a linen cloth over [his] naked [body]. And he remained with him that night, for Jesus taught him the mystery of the kingdom of God. And thence, arising, he returned to the other side of the Jordan.

After these [words] follows the text, 'And James and John come to him,' and all that section. But 'naked [man] with [naked] man' and the other things about which you wrote are not found. And after the [words] 'And he comes into Jericho' [the secret Gospel] adds only, 'And the sister of the youth whom Jesus loved, and his mother and Salome were there, and Jesus did not receive them.' But the many other [things about] which you wrote both seem to be and are falsifications. Now the true explanation and that which accords with the true philosophy ... [The text breaks here in the middle of a page.]

Translation from Morton Smith, *The Secret Gospel: The Discovery and Interpretation of the Secret Gospel According to Mark*, London, Victor Gollancz, 1974.

(v) MISCELLANEA

From the Jewish Talmud:

> Once I was walking along the upper market of Sepphoris and met one [of the disciples of Jesus of Nazareth], who was called Jacob of Kefar Sekanya. He said to me 'It is written in your Law, "You must not bring the earnings of a prostitute into the house of God" (Deuteronomy 23:18). So what was to be done with it – a latrine for the High Priest?'. I did not reply. He said to me, 'Thus Jesus of Nazareth [Yeshu ben Pantera, according to the *Tosefta*] taught me, for they have been collected with prostitutes' earnings, and prostitutes, earnings they will be again (Micah 1:7), they have come from the gutter, and to the gutter they shall return'. And the saying pleased me, and because of this I was arrested.
>
> (*Ab. Zar.* 16b–17a; *T. Hulin* II,24)

From the purported correspondence between James and king Abgar of Edessa:

(a) Abgar's letter to Jesus:

> Abgar Ukkama, the Toparch, to Jesus the good Saviour who has appeared in the district of Jerusalem – greeting.
>
> I have heard concerning you and your cures, how they are accomplished by you without drugs and herbs. For, as the story goes, you make the blind recover their sight, the lame walk, and you cleanse lepers, and cast our unclean spirits and demons, and you cure those who are tortured by long disease and you raise dead men. And when I hear all these things concerning you I decided that it is one of two things, either that you are God and came down from Heaven to do these things, or are the Son of God for doing these things. For this reason I write to beg you to hasten to me and heal the suffering which I have. Moreover I heard that the Jews are mocking you and wish to ill-treat you. Now I have a city very small and venerable which is enough for both of us.

(b) Jesus's reputed reply, via the courier Ananias:

> Blessed are you who believed in me, not having seen me, for it is written concerning me that those who have seen me will not believe in me, and that those who have not seen me will believe and

> live. Now concerning what you wrote to me, to come to you, I must first complete here all for which I was sent, and after thus completing it be taken up to Him who sent me, and when I have been taken up, I will send to you one of my disciples to heal your suffering and give life to you and those with you.
>
> (Translation from J.B. Segal, *Edessa the Blessed City*, pp.61–2)

Words of Jesus as quoted by Addai in the Leningrad manuscript of the *Doctrine of Addai*:

> Accept not anything from any man, and do not own anything in this world.

From the Muslim Qur'ān: A selection of some of the historically unconvincing words attributed to Jesus in the Qur'ān:

> I am the servant of God [Allah]. He has given me the Gospel and ordained me a prophet. His blessing is upon me wherever I go, and He has commanded me to be steadfast in prayer and to give alms to the poor as long as I shall live. He has exhorted me to honour my mother and has purged me of vanity and wickedness. I was blessed on the day I was born, and blessed I shall be on the day of my death; and may peace be upon me on the day when I shall be raised to life.
>
> (Mary sūra)
>
> I am sent forth to you by God to confirm the Torah already revealed and to give news of an apostle that will come after me whose name is Ahmed [an alternative name for Muhammad].
>
> (Battle Array sūra)
>
> 'Jesus, son of Mary', said the disciples, 'can God send down to us from heaven a table spread with food?'.
>
> He replied, 'Have fear of God, if you are true believers'.
>
> 'We wish to eat of it', they said, 'so that we may reassure our hearts and know that what you said to us is true, and that we may be witnesses of it'.
>
> 'Lord', said Jesus, the son of Mary, 'send to us from heaven a table spread with food, that it may mark a feast for us and for those that will come after us: a sign from You. Give us our sustenance. You are the best Giver'.

God replied: 'I am sending one to you. But whoever of you disbelieves hereafter shall be punished as no man has ever been punished'.

Then God will say: 'Jesus, son of Mary, did you ever say to mankind: "Worship me and my mother as gods beside God?"'.

'Glory to You', he will answer, 'how could I say that to which I have no right? If I had ever said so, You would have surely known it. You know what is in my mind, but I cannot tell what is in Yours. You alone know what is hidden. I spoke to them of nothing except that you bade me. I said, "Serve God, my Lord and your Lord". I watched over them while living in their midst, and ever since. You took me to You, You Yourself have been watching over them. You are the witness of all things. They are your own bondsmen: it is for You to punish or to forgive them. You are the Mighty, the Wise One'.

(The Table sūra)
Translations N.J. Dawood, *The Koran*,
Harmondsworth, Penguin, revised ed., 1959

Select Bibliography

Bell, H.I.,
Recent Discoveries of Biblical Papyri,
Oxford, Clarendon Press, 1937.

Bell, H.I., and Skeat, T.C.,
Fragments of an Unknown Gospel,
London, British Museum, 1935.

Churton, Tobias,
The Gnostics,
London, Weidenfeld and Nicolson, 1988.

Cupitt, Don, and Armstrong, Peter,
Who Was Jesus?,
London, BBC, 1977.

Dawood, N.J., (trans.),
The Koran,
Harmondsworth, Penguin, 1959.

Deissman, Adolf,
Light from the Ancient East,
London, Hodder and Stoughton, 1927.

Deuel, Leo,
Testaments of Time, The Story of the Scholar-adventurers and the Search for Lost Manuscripts,
London, Secker and Warburg, 1966.

Doresse, Jean,
Secret Books of the Egyptian Gnostics,
London, Hollis & Carter, 1959.

Dunkerley, Roderic,
Beyond the Gospels,
Harmondsworth, Penguin, 1957.

Eusebius,
The History of the Church,
trans. G.A. Williamson,
Harmondsworth, Penguin, 1965.

Glover, T.R.,
The Jesus of History,
London, SCM Press, 1917.

Grant, Robert M., with Freedman, David Noel,
The Secret Sayings of Jesus According to the Gospel of Thomas,
London, Fontana/Collins, 1960.

Grenfell, B.P.,
'The Oldest Record of Christ. The First Complete Account of the "Sayings of Our Lord"',
intro by F.G. Kenyon,
McClure's, 11, 1897, pp.1022–30.

Grenfell, B.P., and Hunt, A.S., *et al.*,
The Oxyrhynchus Papyri, vols 1–25,
Egypt Exploration Fund, Graeco-Roman Branch, London, 1898–1959.

James, Montague Rhodes,
The Apocryphal New Testament,
Oxford, Clarendon Press, 1924.

Jeremias, J.,
Unknown Sayings of Jesus,
London, SPCK, 1957.

Jones, A., (ed.),
The Jerusalem Bible,
London, Geoffrey Chapman, 1971.

Klausner, Joseph,
Jesus of Nazareth, His Life, Times and Teaching,
(trans.) Herbert Danby,
London, Allen and Unwin, 1928.

Kümmel, W.G.,
Introduction to the New Testament,
(trans.) A.J. Mattill,
London, SCM, 1966.

Metzger, B.,
'Recently published Greek papyri of the New Testament',
Biblical Archaeologist, 10, May 1947, p.38.

Metzger, B.,
Manuscripts of the Greek Bible, An Introduction to Palaeography,
Oxford University Press, 1981.

Pagels, Elaine,
The Gnostic Gospels,
London, Weidenfeld and Nicolson, 1980.

Puech, H.C.,
'Un logion de Jésus sur bandelette funéraire',
Revue de l'Histoire des Religions,
cxlvii, 1955, 126–9.

Quispel, G.,
'The Gospel of Thomas and the New Testament',
Vigiliae Christianae,
XI, 1957, pp.189–207.

Robert, A., and Donaldson, J. (eds.),
The Ante-Nicene Fathers,
Grand Rapids, Eerdmans, 1951, vol VIII.

Robinson, John A.T.,
Redating the New Testament,
London, SCM Press, 1976.

Robinson, J.M.,
The Nag Hammadi Library,
New York, Harper and Row, 3rd revised edition, 1989.

Segal, J.B.,
Edessa the Blessed City,
Oxford, Clarendon Press, 1970.

Sevenster, J.N.,
'Do you know Greek? How much Greek could the first Jewish Christians have known?',
Novum Testamentum,
Suppl. 19, Leiden 1968, pp.3–21.

Smith, Morton,
Clement of Alexandria and a Secret Gospel of Mark,
Harvard University Press, 1973.

Smith, Morton,
The Secret Gospel, The Discovery and Interpretation of the Secret Gospel According to Mark,
London, Gollancz, 1974.

Smith, Robert Houston,
'A sarcophagus from Pella'
Archaeology 26, pp.250–7.

Streeter, B.H.,
The Four Gospels, A Study of Origins,
London, Macmillan, 1927.

Swete, H.B.,
The Akhmim Fragment of the Apocryphal Gospel of St Peter,
London, Macmillan, 1893.

Toynbee, A. (ed.),
The Crucible of Christianity,
London, Thames and Hudson, 1969.

Vermes, Geza,
Jesus the Jew, a Historian's Reading of the Gospels,
London, Collins, 1973.

White, H.G., Evelyn,
The Sayings of Jesus from Oxyrhynchus,
Cambridge, 1920.

Wilkinson, John,
Egeria's Travels,
London, SPCK, 1972.

Wilson, Ian,
Jesus: the Evidence,
London, Weidenfeld and Nicholson, 1984.

Index

NB: *Names with prefixes* al- *and* ben *see under name following*

Acknowledgements

The author wishes to thank the following publishers for permission to reproduce extracts from the following titles in the text:

Allen & Unwin, *Jesus of Nazareth, His Life, Times and Teaching* by J. Klausner; the Clarendon Press, *Recent Discoveries of Biblical Papyri*, by H.I. Bell, *Edessa the Blessed City* by J.B. Segal, *The Apocryphal New Testament* by M.R. James; William Collins, *Jesus the Jew, a Historian's Reading of the Gospels* by G. Vermes; Egypt Exploration Fund, Graeco-Roman Branch, *The Oxyrhynchus Papyri*, vols. 1-25 by B.P. Grenfell and A.S. Hunt *et al*; Fontana, Collins, *The Secret Sayings of Jesus According to the Gospel of Thomas* by R.M. Grant and D.N. Freedman; Harper & Row, New York, *The Nag Hammadi Library* ed. J.M. Robinson; Harvard University Press, *Clement of Alexandria and a Secret Gospel of Mark* by M. Smith; Hodder & Stoughton, U.K., *Light from the Ancient East* by A. Deissman; McClure's, *The Oldest Record Christ. The First Complete Account of the 'Sayings of Our Lord'* by B.P. Grenfell; Oxford University Press, U.S., *Manuscripts of the Greek Bible, An Introduction to Palaeography* by B. Metzger; Penguin Books, *The Koran* trans. N.J. Darwood, *Beyond the Gospels* by R. Dunkerley; *The History of the Church* by Eusebius, trans. G.A. Williams; Society for Promoting Christian Knowledge, *Unknown Sayings of Jesus* by J. Jeremias.

The author also wishes to thank the following for use of the illustrations in the text:

Archaeology, Vol. 26 for Fig. 9; Egypt Exploration Fund for Fig. 3; Mr Ellis H. Minns for Fig.2.